Becoming Your Child's Best Advocate

Printed in the United States of America

First Printing, 2016

ISBN: 978-0-9969169-0-5

Disclaimers

The information in this book is intended for educational use. While author has taken great care in providing current and accurate information, there may be typographical and content errors. The use of these materials, therefore, represents an agreement to hold harmless the author for any liability, claims, damages or expenses that may occur as a result of reliance on information from this book.

Important Notice

You can download a copy of the references, tables and figures and a copy of the sample letters using the following links:

http://themaxwells.org/advocate/references.pdf

http://themaxwells.org/advocate/tables.pdf

http://themaxwells.org/advocate/sample_letters.docx

BECOMING YOUR CHILD'S BEST ADVOCATE:

A Parent's Guide to Helping the Child with Learning Disabilities

Ken Maxwell

INCLUDES CHAPTERS ON FINDING APPROPRIATE SUPPORT
AND ELIMINATING STRESS FOR THE CHILD WITH LEARNING DISABILITIES.

Contents

Acknowledgments

I would first like to thank the parents with whom I worked for eight years as an educational advocate. Their questions, worries, and dedication to finding the right solutions for their children became the framework for *Becoming Your Child's Best Advocate*.

I would also like to thank and acknowledge a number of people who freely gave their time to review and critique chapters of the book:

Jack Kelley—Director of Special Education for his insights about the chapters related to special education regulations and LD self-contained classrooms.

Susan Fino—Former owner of Learning Styles, a private tutoring service for disabled children, for her critique of the chapter on early evaluations. Her comments prompted a shift in focus for early evaluations.

Gail Epstein Mengel—School psychologist and neuropsychologist in private practice, for her detailed analysis of the chapter on testing.

Linda Lafontaine—Speech therapist and principal of The Children's Study Home-Curtis Blake Day School for her insights into the chapter on LD day placements.

I would also like to thank my editors, Corina Koch MacLeod and Carla Douglas of Beyond Paper Editing, for their patience, insights, and so many immediately useful suggestions as *Becoming Your Child's Best Advocate* evolved. As a result of their expert guidance and firsthand knowledge of learning disabilities and parent concerns, *Becoming Your Child's Best Advocate* is a much easier book to read and understand than it was at its inception. They have patiently moved me through an amazing process as a first time author and they have done it with such grace. I am indeed fortunate to have found two professionals who are experts at developmental and copyediting as well as print books and ebooks. It allowed me to have a book that was publisher-ready in both formats.

A special thanks as well to Rebecca Swift, visual artist and cover designer of Rebecca Swift Artwork, who captured the mood and visual effects for the cover of *Becoming Your Child's Best Advocate* with such perfection. It's been a pleasure to work with someone who is so talented.

A special thanks also to professional indexer Sandy Sadow of Sadow Indexing for her excellent work in creating the index for *Becoming Your Child's Best Advocate*. Sandy was very accommodating of my schedule and responded quickly and accurately when I needed the index to complete the book.

Special thanks to those most special to me: -our four children, Kristi, Lynda, Doug, and Mike, for your love and support. To our grandchildren, Adam, Dylan, Erin, Andrew, Missy, Gino, Nick, Katie, Ian and Reilly who are the delight of our lives. To my wife, Diana, for her enthusiastic support as the book evolved and for her love always.

Introduction

Have you ever had any of these feelings about your child's learning disability at home and in your dealings with the school district?

- You were confronted with your child's difficulty completing homework assignment and his* strong reactions to his learning disability.
- You were worried about the impact of your child's lack of progress on her motivation and self-esteem and you believed the school district was not taking those concerns seriously.
- You were frustrated that the school district seemed content to continue the same services in spite of your child's lack of progress.
- You were upset that your requests for increased services were refused

If you have had any of these feelings, you're not alone. In fact, they occur to most parents much of the time. How do I know that? I know it from being present in hundreds of meetings with parents as a professional educator and as an educational advocate over a period of 40 years.

In *Becoming Your Child's Best Advocate*, you'll learn how to properly address the negative impact that having a learning disability (LD) is having on your child's learning and self-esteem. You'll discover how your genuine positive feelings, coupled with intense services, can shift your child's outlook to help her become productive and successful in school and in other areas of life.

When a parent knows that their child is LD, they will typically find out as much as they can about learning disabilities and their potential impact on the child. That knowledge is necessary and useful. However, most of the texts on LD won't answer the many questions you'll have when you first refer your child for special education, when they've been given an individual education program (IEP), or when you want to consider a change of placement to an LD self-contained program in your district or a day school. You might have some of these questions:

How do I properly prepare for an initial evaluation where the school district uses either response to intervention (RTI), a severe discrepancy, or a pattern of strengths and weaknesses to determine eligibility?

What information can I gather and review in advance of a meeting that will help me feel confident about the outcome?

What skills and training are needed by an advocate or attorney that will be most helpful to me if I ask them to attend an initial evaluation or re-evaluation, or to request an increase in services or placement in an LD self-contained program or an LD day school? How do I find such a person?

How can I know whether the advocate or attorney I hire is the right match for me?

How can I increase my chances of success when I request an increase in my child's services or a change of placement?

How can I know whether an LD self-contained program in my district or an LD day school is right for my child?

Becoming Your Child's Best Advocate introduces four foundation chapters:

- understanding testing,
- understanding both federal and your state's special education regulations,
- collecting information, and
- finding proper support.

These chapters will give you the background knowledge needed to properly prepare for any meeting you attend.

In the remaining chapters, you'll also learn how to apply your foundation knowledge in initial evaluations and re-evaluations, to request an increase in services and placement in an LD self-contained program in your district or an LD day placement.

When your child is not making adequate progress, *Becoming Your Child's Best Advocate* will help you carefully consider whether (and when) to ask for increased services or a change of placement. Whichever one you choose, you'll learn how to build a strong case so that you won't have to make your request a second or third time.

Whether you're new to special education or you're a veteran, you'll have access to useful information to help you solve the most challenging problems parents face. You can also use *Becoming Your Child's Best Advocate* as a reference at any point during your child's time in special education.

As you read *Becoming Your Child's Best Advocate*, you'll increase your knowledge and learn how to eliminate or significantly reduce your child's stress about her LD. It's my goal that this combination will free you to attend meetings feeling relaxed and confident and with the conviction that what you're doing is the right thing for your child. I truly want you to be your child's best advocate, and I believe *Becoming Your Child's Best Advocate* will allow you to do that.

*Note that throughout the book when I refer to a child, I've used the pronouns "he," "him," and "his" in even-numbered chapters, and "she," "her," and "hers" in odd-numbered chapters. In the Introduction, I've alternated between them.

Abbreviations

ADD — attention deficit disorder

ADHD — attention deficit hyperactivity disorder

BMP — behavior management program

CBA — curriculum-based assessment

CBM — curriculum-based measurement

IDEA — Individuals with Disabilities Education Act

IEE — independent educational evaluation

IEP — individual education program

LD — learning disability

NCLB — No Child Left Behind

PLOP — present level of performance

PSW — pattern of strengths and weaknesses

RTI — response to intervention

SD — standard deviation

Chapter 1
Understanding Your Child's Stress

You have this incredible ability to use your thoughts and feelings (your beliefs) to help your child be productive and successful in school and other areas of their life.

It may seem unusual to have the first chapter of a book about learning disabilities (LD) to be on the topic of stress. My experience as a counselor, school psychologist, administrator of special education, and educational advocate, however, convinced me that it was very appropriate. It was appropriate because I found that children's stress about their LD was universally present by third grade if they were not receiving services consistent with their needs.

It's such an important topic because stress has the potential to create a lifelong avoidance of skills that are essential for your child to be productive and successful as an adult. Unfortunately, many children with LD are not identified until third grade or beyond. If that's the case with your child, you will already be dealing with her stress about learning skills as well as her belief about how she's viewed by her peers.

Note: Throughout the book when I refer to a child, I've used the pronouns "he," "him,", and "his," in even-numbered chapters, and "she," "her," and "hers" in odd numbered chapters.

A clear plan of action will be needed to turn that around. That plan must focus on getting intense services while at the same time preventing (if your child is in first or second grade) or significantly reducing (if she is in third grade or beyond) your child's stress about her LD. That, in turn, will free her to focus on being successful in school instead of

1

being preoccupied with negative thoughts and feelings. Let's look at how you can do that.

The Evolution and Impact of Negative Beliefs

Beliefs are formed from our feelings about the events we experience in our daily lives. The feelings we have will typically go through a slow evolution over a period of time before becoming a belief.

Negative beliefs form when we repeatedly experience an event as undesirable. For example, your child may form a negative belief about riding a bike if she isn't successful after repeated attempts at trying to learn.

As a result of her belief, she'll avoid riding a bike and will resist any further invitation to learn, even when it may have a negative impact on her friendships. Your child's experience with her LD will go through a similar evolution.

From Excitement to Negative Feelings

Your child will usually be excited about going to school and will start out with positive feelings. This will be particularly so if she has older brothers or sisters, as it will allow her to feel "grown up" too.

However, if your child isn't mastering skills and doesn't receive intensive help, her feelings will gradually shift from positive to negative between the first and third grade.

Most children with learning disabilities will do a good job of hiding their emotions in school. Others may display them, but it will usually be at a point where their LD is already having a significant impact on learning.

Negative Feelings Create Avoidance

As a result of your child's discovery that she has weak skills (LD), which occurs frequently by third grade, you may see changes in behavior at home. Your child may

- act out or withdraw,
- avoid work in her weak skills,
- complain that the work is too hard,
- make comments such as "I'm stupid" or "I'm dumb," or
- tell you she's sick to avoid going to school or become "sick" at school to be sent home.

By the time your child is in fifth grade or beyond, comments about school will most likely sound something like "the work is stupid" or "the teacher is stupid." The older child may also avoid work in her weak skills by "forgetting it" at school, or she may bring it home and then not complete it.

Avoidance Attracts Negative Beliefs

Unless there's appropriate help, your child's avoidance and awareness that she has weak skills will become a belief, and we know that once a belief is formed it will have a powerful effect on learning. To understand this better, let's suppose that your child's weakness is in reading.

In first grade, your child will have difficulty with reading but will usually not be aware of its significance because all of her peers will be learning beginning reading skills as well. Even though some children will be ahead of her, she's not likely to pay much attention to that difference.

It's when the pace increases in second grade and the curriculum shifts away from beginning reading in third grade, that your child is most likely to become aware that she's not performing like others. If she's like most children with LD, she'll form a negative belief such as "I'm not good at reading."

The belief that she's not good at reading can then impact her progress in any of the following ways: She may

- hide her work from her classmates because she believes she'll be teased;
- pretend she's finished reading in-class reading assignments by the teacher in order to look like the other students;
- worry that she'll be asked to read out loud and feel highly stressed if she's asked to read;
- believe that she will have difficulty any time she has to perform in reading;
- object to leaving the room to receive extra help because she believes it will make her look different;
- avoid reading for pleasure;
- avoid reading homework;
- believe she won't perform well on classroom tests, state tests or on college board exams in her weak skills;
- choose courses in high school that are less challenging because she believes she won't perform well;
- choose courses in high school or college that are below her potential;
- decide to drop out because school is having such a negative impact on her self-esteem; or
- choose a career that is below her potential.

Consequences of Negative Beliefs

If your child's weak reading skills are not addressed, the belief that she's not good at reading will result in poor performance, and that will further reinforce her belief, thus creating a cycle of poor performance.

There's often a second effect as well. Your child may start to believe that because she can't perform in reading, she must be stupid, even though that will be far from the truth.

The above list points out something important about beliefs: a belief will have a greater impact on your child's learning than her disability. I say that because we know that with intensive help, your child can learn a basic skill. A belief, however, will be much more resistant to change once it's established.

In our reading example, this means your child's belief (her stress) about not performing well in reading will be there any time reading is required in school or at home. The longer it goes without being addressed, the greater the impact it will have on her learning, and in all probability, her self-image.

Preventing a Negative Belief

Are there ways to prevent your child from forming a negative belief about her LD and a negative self-image? Yes, there are. One way is to make sure your child receives intensive help early—in first or second grade. Early help will provide a successful experience, giving her a feeling of confidence about her learning.

Once your child starts to experience success in a skill, she'll form the belief that she's good at that skill. Her belief in success will result in successful performance, and that will further reinforce her belief, creating a cycle of successful experiences. Her success will also allow her to feel that she can master skills like her peers—that she's smart.

Your child's belief that she's successful won't change her LD. She'll continue to need intensive help with her weak skill(s) until they approach grade level. What will be different is that she'll automatically put in the necessary time and effort to be successful because she believes she's successful. The idea that she might have difficulty won't occur to her.

Other Sources of Support

Another way you can help your child—which I'm sure you're already aware of—is to support any natural talent she has. It's important for her to have as many areas of success as possible, to offset any negative feelings she has about her performance in specific skills.

Let's not forget tutoring after school or during the summer. Look for a highly experienced, enthusiastic professional who will ensure that your child experiences success right from their first contact.

How Parents Influence Their Child's Beliefs

The Impact of a Belief in Struggle

Some parents carry the belief that their child will struggle with their LD. That's a natural reaction, especially if the parent struggled in school or someone else in the family struggles with LD. Without realizing it, however, you will add to your child's stress if you carry that belief.

Your child will then be dealing with the reality of her LD and in addition will "take on" your belief that she will struggle if she's young. If she's older, it can act as a barrier to her progress.

The same thing will happen for any other belief you carry about your child's LD, such as a belief that she may not be able to attend college, or that she may not lead a productive life. The good news is that you can help to prevent your child from forming a belief in struggle, and you can help to change her belief if it's already formed. Let's take a look at how that can happen.

Carrying a Genuine Belief in Success

To prevent a belief in struggle (or to begin to change it if your child already has a belief in struggle), you can shift to carrying a genuine belief that your child is successful in school and other areas of her life. Notice that you frame your belief in the present tense. We say, "my child *is* successful," not "*will be* successful." That's so your intention for her to be successful will have impact immediately, not at some point in the future. When I refer to a genuine belief, I'm not referring to your intellectual understanding of your child's success. Your genuine belief must be heartfelt for it to have impact.

It's not necessary to tell your child you believe in her success. All you need to do is carry a genuine belief and she will know it. Also, notice that your genuine belief is stated in general terms, so that your child will carry a belief that she's successful in all areas of her life.

Although it's not necessary to tell your child you believe in her success, it is important to support her efforts with praise and encouragement, particularly before and during the time she's receiving intensive help.

Your child needs a champion, and your positive feedback is essential all the way through school. You also hope there will be teachers, tutors and coaches who are "champions" as well.

Although we're focusing on the child with LD, it's important to carry your genuine belief in success for all of your children. I say that because I'm sure you realize that children who do not have a learning disability can also form a belief that they're not good at a skill.

Think about how many friends you have who do not have a learning disability who have told you confidentially that they avoid reading, writing, or math because of early experiences that convinced them they could not perform well in those skills.

You're truly giving a beautiful gift to all of your children by carrying a genuine belief in their success. Although your belief will have a positive effect at any age, it will have the greatest impact when they're young. In fact, you should begin this as soon as they're born, and never stop.

A Belief in Struggle vs. a Belief in Success

There's a big difference between a child who approaches a subject believing it will be difficult (she will struggle) and one who approaches that same subject believing she will be successful. Let's look at each.

Suppose your child holds the belief that she will struggle in reading. That means she will be anxious (stressed) about reading any time she has to perform in that subject. She will anticipate that any aspect of reading, including learning a new skill in reading, reading a passage and answering questions, reading orally, or taking a test, will be difficult.

Your child's belief in struggle will lead to poor performance and will reinforce her belief that reading is difficult. She's very likely to avoid reading as a result. Her avoidance, in turn, will cause her to fall even further behind her peers. If she's receiving intensive help, her belief in struggle will slow down her progress.

If your child believes she will be successful in reading, she will anticipate success with any aspect of reading she encounters. Her belief in success will lead to good performance and will reinforce her belief that she's successful. If she's receiving intensive help, her belief in success will accelerate her progress and allow her to feel optimistic about it as well.

Your child's belief in success and intensive help go together. If one is missing, it can have a significant impact on her progress and self-esteem.

Changing a Belief in Struggle

Shifting to a genuine belief in success may not happen automatically if you have carried a belief in struggle for some time. You'll need to be patient. However, removing your belief in struggle and shifting to a belief in success, coupled with intensive help, will allow your child to change her belief to an optimistic view about school and about herself.

Note: If you do not carry a belief in struggle, focus on getting intensive help for your child supported by your belief in her success.

As your child makes progress, the negative behaviors you were seeing at home and those that were present in school will start to diminish. That will tell you that your child is starting to shift to a belief in success. Your genuine belief in her success will support her newly found confidence.

You will know that there's a significant shift when your child begins to take on homework and other school projects on her own. You'll be witnessing the effect of her mastery of skills and her belief in success.

Addressing Exceptions

I said earlier that one of the keys to preventing a negative belief from forming is your child's referral in first or second grade. The teacher may not agree with a referral. What do you do?

You'll have two choices. The first is to collect information about your child for a brief period (several months) and then refer her. The second is to have your child evaluated privately. We'll discuss both of these options in chapter 4.

What about the child in third grade or beyond who may already have formed a belief about her learning and perhaps her ability, too? The key again is for your child to receive intensive help, preferably in third or fourth grade, coupled with your belief in her success.

An older child may also need a period of counseling, supported by your belief, until she begins to experience success in school. If you use a school counselor, I recommend requesting a social worker. If your child is in elementary school, the principal will have information about who to contact. If your child is in middle or high school, the guidance department will have this information.

Key Concepts

You can address your child's negative beliefs by

- getting intensive help for your child any time after the middle of first grade;
- being aware of how your beliefs might influence your child's beliefs;
- carrying a genuine belief in your child's success;
- focusing on what your child can do;

- supporting your child's natural talents; and
- providing additional support through tutoring.

Looking Ahead

Your genuine belief in your child's success, coupled with intensive help, is critical to support her confidence in learning new skills. In addition to your love, it's one of the most important gifts you can give her as she moves through the grades and into later life.

Doing your part to prevent or change negative beliefs is one of the most useful skills you can learn if you're going to be your child's best advocate.

The coming chapters focus on increasing your knowledge. As you read them, you'll be reminded to use your new skills, which will help you to have a positive outcome in all of your interactions with the school district. Look for the Stress Check at the end of each chapter.

The next four chapters will focus on understanding test reports, how special education regulations will be used to determine your child's eligibility in the LD category, collecting information for team meetings, and finding appropriate support.

Once you have that foundation knowledge, I'll show you how to apply it to any meeting you attend. You'll discover how easy it is to know where you want to focus your energy. Then you'll truly begin to understand what helping your child be successful coupled with increasing your knowledge mean.

For those who are new to special education, I suggest you read through the four chapters, keeping in mind that you'll be applying the foundation skills to the remaining chapters in this book. In that way, your knowledge will become second nature to you. The best approach is to relax and simply absorb the material. You'll find it will all come back to you as you use it.

For those who are special education pros, I recommend reading all of the chapters as well. You may know some of the content already, but it will be presented differently and you'll find new information to think about. Reading the chapters will also help you to see how to apply the foundation skills in a step-by-step way.

Chapter 2
Understanding Test Scores Presented at Team Meetings

Once you have taken the steps to understand something, you'll find that fear was the only thing holding you back—not lack of skill or ability.

Becoming Comfortable with Test Results

Parents talk to me about how uncomfortable they feel at IEP meetings. One reason this happens is that they feel they lack the knowledge the professionals at the meeting have about testing. As you review this foundation chapter, you'll find that test reports are actually quite easy to understand once you learn a few of the basic rules. You'll also be able to apply your knowledge to most of the test reports you read, regardless of the professional reporting at a meeting.

There are also some parents who avoid informing themselves about testing because they believe it will involve a lot of mathematics. The only mathematics you'll have to know in this chapter is how to add or subtract. Instead of math calculation, you'll learn what test scores mean. Your new knowledge will make a significant difference when you attend IEP meetings. You'll be able to relax, knowing you have the same understanding of your child's reports as other team members. With that new comfort level, you can focus on being your child's best advocate. We'll first take a look at the major types of tests used and then discuss how to properly interpret test scores.

Criterion-Referenced Tests

Criterion-referenced tests in schools are used to determine your child's progress and knowledge in curriculum areas like reading, writing, spelling, and mathematics. Scores are usually reported as a number or percent of correct responses, such as getting a numerical score of 75 out of 100 on a spelling test or 80 percent on a math test.

The test makers as well as the professionals who work in schools use criteria (standards) for success on most tests. For example, a teacher might want all of the children in her class to have test scores of 80 or better to determine that they're mastering material in reading comprehension. So the criterion for success in reading comprehension would be 80.

The special education teacher will also require your child to meet certain criteria for success in special education. These will be found in the goals and objectives of his IEP. For example, an annual goal in reading fluency (your child's reading rate and accuracy) might be for him to improve reading fluency from 40 to 100 words per minute. The criterion for success in reading fluency would be 100 words per minute.

Criterion-referenced tests don't compare your child to other students; they measure your child's progress and knowledge and tell you if he's meeting a specific criterion for success. Criterion-referenced tests are usually given frequently during a school year to document your child's progress, such as the tests and quizzes your child takes that later become report card grades.

Progress Monitoring

There's a special kind of criterion-referenced testing that's now being used frequently called progress monitoring. Progress monitoring is the testing component of response to intervention (RTI), an approach some school districts use to identify and provide extra help for students who are at risk of failure.

Progress monitoring is a relatively new term. Another name for it is curriculum-based measurement (CBM). It's different from most criterion-referenced tests because it uses standardized procedures to create, administer, score, and interpret its tests. That means its results will be reliable and valid.

Reliability means that a test is dependable; it will give similar results from one test administration to the next. Validity means that a test measures what it claims to measure. Most criterion-referenced tests are not reliable or valid.

Progress monitoring is designed with multiple tests that can be given frequently (once a week or once every two weeks) to monitor your child's progress. The tests are samples of the curriculum for kindergarten through eighth grade and take five minutes or less to administer. The results are frequently put on graphs, making it very easy for you to follow your child's progress.

Figure 2.1 is a graph of Mason's progress in reading fluency measured in words read correctly per minute (see vertical scale on the left hand side of the chart) over a period of 24 weeks of instruction.

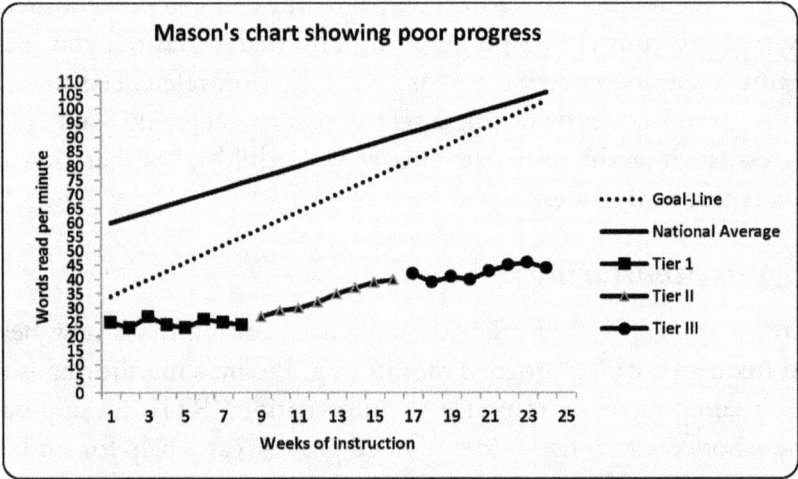

Figure 2.1. Mason's progress monitoring chart showing poor progress

The three lines for tiers I, II, and III (they may also be called primary, secondary and tertiary levels) are Mason's weekly scores in reading fluency (RTI typically has three tiers of instruction with the intensity of services increasing with each tier). Each tier is usually eight weeks.

Mason also has a goal line (the dotted line). The top of the goal line represents the score in reading fluency he's expected to achieve by the end of the year and is the same as his reading fluency goal in his IEP. Mason's goal line is set in this example so he'll be at the level of his peers nationally by the end of the year (see solid line for national average).

Note: A national average (comparing your child to others at his grade or age level across the country) may not be reported on some progress charts. In that case, you'll compare your child to others nationally using the results from standardized tests, which we'll discuss next.

To be satisfied that he's making enough progress, Mason's teacher would like his scores in reading fluency to be at or above the goal line. The change of tiers at weeks 8 and 16 (see space between tiers) indicates that the teacher was not satisfied with his progress and made changes in the method of instruction.

That usually means that the teacher has either increased the amount of time per week that Mason will receive instruction and/or has decreased the size of the group he's in. Mason's progress over 24 weeks of instruction shows that he didn't make significant gains. Since he failed to make progress, it's very likely that he'll be recommended for a special education evaluation.

Noah's progress chart in figure 2.2 is more encouraging. Notice how his scores increased rapidly in Tier III. It appears that with continued help he'll meet his goal for the year and will be at the level of his peers nationally. He won't need to be referred for special education.

Graphing progress this way is easy to understand and gives you clear, objective evidence you can use to make decisions. Not all school districts use progress monitoring, however, and it's used most often in regular education.

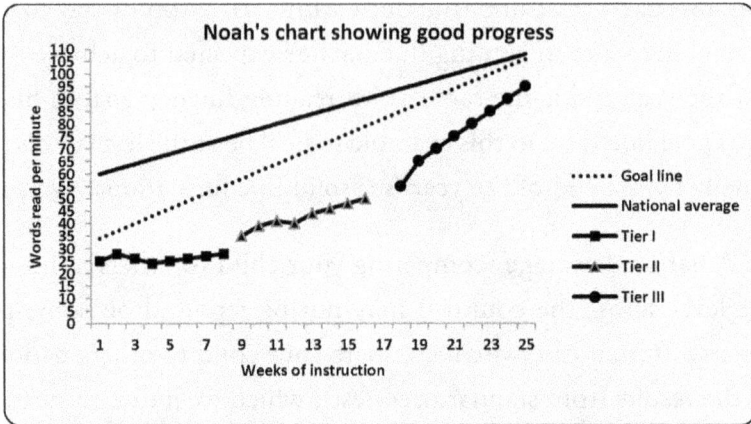

Figure 2.2. Noah's progress monitoring chart showing good progress

Source: Adapted from the Colorado Department of Education. (2008) Guidelines for Identifying Students with Specific Learning Disabilities Denver, CO: Author. Available at http://www.cde.state.co.us/sites/default/files/documents/cdesped/download/pdf/sld_guidelines.pdf

Standardized Tests

Standardized tests (also called norm-referenced tests) compare your child to other children at the same age and grade level. You learned earlier that with the exception of progress monitoring, or CBM, most criterion-referenced tests have no established reliability or validity. Standardized tests, however, are reliable and valid.

In fact, the companies that develop standardized tests for schools spend a great deal of time making sure their tests are reliable and valid. They do so because they want to provide an accurate picture of your child's performance.

Most standardized tests are given once a year. They can be used to compare your child to other children at his grade level, across your district, to other students in your state, or to students nationally.

Interpreting Standardized Test Scores

The descriptions of test scores that follow are the different ways standardized test scores are reported in special education. They're used to report scores in all basic skill areas (reading, writing, spelling, and math). They may also be used to report scores for behavior and social skills (not covered here).

It will help you to understand our discussion if you refer to table 2.1.

Table 2.1 has four scores from left to right, as follows: z-scores, standard scores, percentiles, and scaled scores. Most of the test reports you receive will report scores as standard scores and percentiles. Scaled scores will be reported less frequently.

In testing, z-scores are used to show how far a score is from the mean or average score. As you'll see, z-scores will help you understand how your child compares to the typical peer at his grade level.

Standard Scores

Most of the tests used by professionals who evaluate children and adolescents have standard scores with a mean (also called an average score) of 100 and a standard deviation of 15. A standard deviation tells how spread-out a group of scores is from the mean.

Notice that standard deviations (SD) are shown in the z-score column in table 2.1. That's because z-scores are converted to SD so they remain in the column with z-scores.

One standard deviation above the mean (+1SD) on your table corresponds to a standard score of 115 (100 + 15) and one standard deviation below the mean (-1SD) corresponds to a standard score of 85 (100-15). Scores between 85 and 115 are considered to be in the average range. Most students in your child's grade (about 68 percent) will score in the average range.

Table 2.1 Test scores used frequently in special education				
Z- Scores	Standard	Percentile	Scaled	Description
	Score	Rank	Score	
+3.0 SD	145	99	19	Very superior
	140	99	18	
	135	99	17	
+2.0 SD	130	98	16	
	125	95	15	Superior
	120	91	14	
+1.0 SD	115	84	13	High Average
	110	75	12	
	105	65	11	Average
0.0 SD	100	50	10	
	95	38	9	
	90	25	8	
- 1.0 SD	85	16	7	Low Average
	80	9	6	
- 1.5 SD	77	6	5	Weak
	75	5	5	
- 2.0 SD	70	2	4	
	65	1	3	Exceptionally Weak
	60	>1	2	
- 3.0 SD	55	>1	1	

A score below 90 on table 2.1 will tell you that your child is having difficulty mastering the skills at his grade level for the particular skill area in which he's tested. The lower the standard score, the fewer skills he has mastered. For example, if he has a standard score of 80 on a test of sight words (described as low average on table 2.1), it means he's having difficulty mastering the skills in that area of reading.

A standard score above 115 on your table means that your child has mastered many of the skills at his grade level for the skill area in which he's tested. The higher the standard score, the more skills he's mastered.

When you're looking at standardized tests that have a mean of 100 and an SD of 15, you should consider 90 or above the score you want your child to achieve. That will tell you that his skills are at grade level.

Tests frequently used to measure basic skills achievement in special education are the Wechsler Individual Achievement Test (WIAT III) and the Woodcock–Johnson Psycho-Educational Battery (WJ III).

Closing the Gap in Skills

Standard scores are an excellent way to know if your child is catching up to his peers (closing the gap in skills). When standard scores drop from one year to the next, it will tell you that your child is falling further behind his peers. On the other hand, if his scores increase, it means he's catching up to his peers.

Let's look at an example. Table 2.2 shows Matthew's test scores in reading using subtests from the Wechsler Individual Achievement Test (WIAT II).

Table 2.2 Matthew's gap in skills documenting regression				
Reading	Grade 3 4/24/13	Grade 4 4/26/14		
Subtest name	Standard score	Standard score	Difference	Description
Word reading	80	72	- 8	Has not closed the gap in skills
Reading comprehension	80	80	0	Has made one year of growth but has not closed the gap in skills
Pseudoword decoding	78	88	+10	Has closed the gap in skills

You'll see that his scores in word reading from third to fourth grade dropped from 80 to 72, a decrease of eight points. He's not closing the gap in skills for word reading—he's falling further behind his peers.

His scores for reading comprehension stayed the same, however. When a child's standard scores stay the same for two consecutive years of testing, it's interpreted as a gain of one year in skills. Since the typical peer in his class will also have gained one year in skills, however, your child will not be closing the gap in skills.

To close the gap, Matthew would have to gain more than one year in skills. This means that he would need a score of 81 or greater to close the gap in reading comprehension. Matthew has gained 10 points in pseudoword decoding and he is closing the gap in that area of reading.

When a student has not closed the gap in skills, as in Mathew's word reading, we refer to it as regression. Any time your child regresses in a skill, you'll want to have the team look closely at why that's happening. If there's not a reasonable explanation, you should request an increase in services in that skill area. We'll discuss requesting an increase in services in chapter 9.

Tip: You can compare standard scores for any standardized test and in any basic skill where the mean and standard deviation are the same. Most tests used with the special education population will have a mean of 100 and a standard deviation of 15.

Just make sure you're comparing scores from the same tests when you make these calculations. For example, if the test used one year for mathematics was the Wechsler Individual Achievement Test (WIAT II) you want to make sure that the WIAT II was used the second year too, so you're comparing apples to apples.

Note: The Roman numeral after a test name refers to the latest published version of that test. So, if a test changes from II to III, the higher number is the latest version.

Percentiles

Percentiles have a range of 1 to 99 with a mean of 50. The 16th percentile on table 2.1 is 1 SD below the mean, and the 84th percentile is 1 SD above the mean. The 16th and 84th percentiles are shown as -1 SD and +1 SD on your table. Percentiles between 16 and 84 are considered to be in the average range.

A score below the 25th percentile will tell you that your child is having difficulty mastering the skills at his grade level for the particular skill area in which he's tested. The lower the percentile, the fewer skills he's mastered. For example, if he scored at the 6th percentile on a test of math division (described as weak on table 2.1), it means he's having difficulty mastering the skills in that area of math.

Scores above the 84th percentile mean that your child has mastered many of the skills at his grade level for the skill area in which he's tested. The higher the percentile, the more skills he's mastered.

When you're looking at percentiles for standardized tests, you should consider the 25th percentile or above to be the score you want your child to achieve. That will tell you his skills are at grade level.

The Wechsler Individual Achievement Test and the Woodcock–Johnson Battery, which I discussed earlier, report scores as percentiles as well as standard scores. These tests are frequently used by schools to test children and adolescents because they're respected by experts in the field and they're comprehensive.

They test students from kindergarten to twelfth grade in all basic skill areas. That's nice, because it means that the same test can be used as long as your child is in special education. It will help you to make the kind of comparisons you need to, from year to year, to determine if your child is closing the gap in skills.

Scaled Scores

Another score used in testing is a scaled score. You'll see in table 2.1 that scaled scores have a range of 1 to 19. A scaled score of 10 is average. A scaled score of 7 is one standard deviation below the mean (-1SD) and a scaled score of 13 is one standard deviation above the mean (+1SD).

When you're looking at scaled scores for standardized tests, you should consider 8 or above the score you want your child to achieve. That will tell you his scores are at grade level. The Wechsler Individual Achievement Test described earlier also reports scores as scaled scores.

Avoiding Confusion

Don't confuse standard scores or percentiles with report card grades. A grade on a report card is usually an average score from a number of tests, each with a range of 0 to 100, with 100 being the highest grade possible. A score of 85 on a report card, therefore, is considered a good grade. Report card grades don't compare your child to other students.

A standard score of 85 on a standardized test is low average (see table 2.1) because it's 15 points below the mean of 100 (remember that standard scores range from 55 to 145, with 100 being an average score, not the highest possible score). Standard scores compare your child to others at his age and grade level.

A percentile of 85 described as high average on table 2.1 tells you that your child has scored the same as or better than 85 percent of the students who took the same test. Percentiles also compare your child to others at their age and grade level. Although a report card grade, a standard score, and a percentile may have the same numerical score, each has a different meaning.

Understanding Composite, Cluster, and Total Scores

Some of the test reports you receive will have scores called composite or cluster scores. Composite or cluster scores are calculated by combining scores for each section of a test.

The Wechsler Individual Achievement Test, the Woodcock–Johnson Psycho-Educational Battery and the Wechsler Intelligence Scale for Children are the most common tests using composite or cluster scores. The Wechsler Intelligence Scale calls their composite scores Index Scores.

They're useful because they give a total for each major skill area tested such as a total for all reading or math subtests. Table 2.3 is an example of composite and cluster scores using the Wechsler Individual Achievement Test (WIAT II) standard scores and percentiles.

Table 2.3 Daniel's test profile showing composite and total scores		
Wechsler Individual Achievement Test (WIAT II) Grade 3		
Subtest	Standard Score	Percentile
Reading		
Word reading	80	9
Reading comprehension	119	89
Pseudoword decoding	84	14
Composite score	92	29
Mathematics		
Numerical operations	106	65
Math reasoning	118	88
Composite score	113	81
Written language		
Spelling	74	4
Written expression	84	14
Composite score	78	6
Oral Language		
Listening comprehension	117	86
Oral expression	123	93
Composite score	124	94
Total	98	46

When you look at test scores, it's important to look at all of the scores carefully. For example, Daniel's reading Composite Score of 92 (29th percentile) is in the average range. You recall that standard scores between 85 and 115 (16 and 84 percentile) in Table 2.1 are average. Notice, however, that in Table 2.3, Daniel's Reading Comprehension subtest score is high average (119) while Word Reading (80) and Pseudoword Reading (84) are both low average scores. It's important, therefore, to look beyond the composite scores to get a true picture of how your child is doing.

The same applies to a Total Score. A Total score is calculated by combining all of the composite scores on a test. Daniel's Total Score of 98 (46th percentile) is average. However, the total is misleading because he has high average (113) to superior (124) composite scores for Mathematics and Oral Language and a weak score for Written Language (78).

When you look at test scores, remember that a score below 90 (25th percentile) tells you that skills in the area tested have not been mastered. The lower the score the fewer skills have been mastered. With this in mind, Daniel will require help mastering skills in reading, spelling and written expression.

Note: When you identify a low score on a test (below 90, 25 or 8), you should always look for confirmation of that weak score from another standardized test and other relevant information such as a teacher's comments at a meeting or a work sample. I'll show you how to do this in the coming chapters.

You should also be aware that some test reports you receive will use different scores to show below average performance than the ones we've been discussing (scores below 90, 25 or 8). If it's not clear in a test report, ask the evaluator what scores on that test (standard scores, percentiles or scaled scores) will tell you your child's performance is below average.

Summary of Standardized Test Scores

Table 2.4 is a summary of our discussion about standardized test scores. In the first column, standard scores below those shown will tell you that your child is not mastering skills. The lower the score, the fewer the skills he will have mastered.

Table 2.4 Summary of standardized test scores		
Scores used frequently in special education testing	Scores below those shown will tell you your child is not mastering skills	Scores at or above those shown will tell you your child's skills are at the level of a typical peer
Standard scores	90	90
Percentiles	25	25
Scaled scores	8	8

The second column shows the scores that will tell you your child's skills are at the level of his peers. You can use table 2.4 as a guide when you review your district or a private evaluator's standardized test results.

Scores below those in the first column will tell you that your child is going to need extra support. That support may come from special education, regular education, or it may come from private tutoring.

It's important to understand that each state or school district will use its own standards (criteria) for entry into special education. Some districts will use different standards than those shown in table 2.4. For example, your district may use standard scores of 77, percentiles of 6 and scaled scores of 5 as their entry criteria. If you look at table 2.1, you'll see that those scores are 1.5 SD below the mean.

That means there will be students who will not qualify for special education even though they may not be mastering skills and will need extra support. If that should happen, you will want consider one of the following options:

- An independent educational evaluation (IEE) discussed in chapter 3.
- A regular education remedial program in your district in reading, math, or writing. You can read more about what you should look for in a remedial program in appendix IV.

- A private summer program
- Private tutoring

Each of the above options will be discussed in more detail in chapter 7.

Congratulations! You have just completed a mini-course in understanding testing. It really isn't as complicated as it first looks, is it? Re-read this chapter if you need a little more time to digest the information. Now you can review your child's test results before an evaluation meeting and know what the scores mean when criterion-referenced tests (including progress monitoring) and standardized test results are discussed.

Key Concepts

To understand test results, you will need to

- be aware how criterion-referenced tests are used;
- be familiar with progress monitoring, the testing component of RTI;
- know how to interpret standardized test results;
- know how to determine if your child is closing the gap in skills;
- avoid confusing report card grades with standard scores and percentiles; and
- understand how composite scores are used.

Stress Check

Are you feeling more comfortable after reading this chapter? You now have a way to know how well your child is doing. For example, you can compare the standard scores from two years of testing to determine if your child is closing the gap in skills or is regressing (see table 2.2). And you know which standardized scores on a test will tell you that your child is not mastering skills or when he's at the level of his peers (see table 2.4).

You can also use progress monitoring results the same way. The chart(s) you receive on your child's progress (similar to Mason's and Noah's progress charts at the beginning of the chapter) will tell you clearly how well he's doing.

You may also have questions about some of the school district's reports that you'll receive before your child's IEP meeting. If you're using an advocate or private evaluator, they can help you.

However, if you're attending a meeting alone or with a friend, you'll want to have your questions answered before your meeting. That will mean speaking to the professional whose report you have questions about.

Resist the temptation to interpret something in a report before you speak to a professional. They may have an entirely different explanation of that information.

You should not walk into a meeting still worried or uncomfortable. You want to do everything you can to reduce any stress you may have before a meeting takes place. That will free you to use the knowledge from this and the coming chapters to be relaxed and focused on what you need to do. Let's look at the second foundation skill.

Chapter 3
Understanding the Individuals with Disabilities Education Act

You want have the highest level of respect for your rights. You want them there for your child and for their children as well.

Special Education Originates at the Federal Level

In chapter 2, I focused on increasing your knowledge about test scores. It's equally important for you to understand how the IEP team will decide if your child qualifies for special education in the learning disability category and the types of meetings you will attend once your child has an IEP. You'll also need to know what to do if a team denies your request to evaluate your child or if your child is found not eligible for special education.

For that, we turn to the federal special education regulations called the Individuals with Disabilities Education Act (IDEA). IDEA serves as a blueprint that all states must follow to write their special education regulations. Some sections of the federal regulations must be followed exactly as they are written. Other sections give states some flexibility.

The last major change in the federal special education regulations occurred 11 years ago. IDEA identified eight requirements that IEP teams must use to determine eligibility in the LD category. Four of these (2, 3, 4A, and 4B, below) give states or school districts options. They may choose one or more when they consider eligibility for special education.

What follows is a summary of those requirements. For the exact language of the regulations you can log onto http://www.parentcenterhub.org/repository/partb-subpartd/#300.307.

The Essence of IDEA's Requirements

1. There must be evidence that your child is not achieving adequately relative to your child's age or state-approved grade- level standards in one or more of the following areas:

- oral expression,
- listening comprehension,
- written expression,
- basic reading skills (phonemic awareness, phonics, and vocabulary),
- reading fluency,
- reading comprehension,
- mathematics calculation, and
- mathematics problem solving.

Comment: IDEA does not define what "achieving adequately" means. That decision is left to each state. Some states define it for all school districts. Others provide guidance about what it means and allow school districts to establish their own standards for achieving adequately. It's typical to use standardized achievement tests to determine adequate achievement.

Notice that spelling is not included in the list of skills. This means you can't refer your child for spelling only. However, you can refer her for spelling in combination with written expression.

2. There must be evidence that your child is not making sufficient progress to meet age or state-approved grade-level standards in one or more of the basic skills identified in item 1, above, when using a process based on scientific, research-based intervention.

Comment: Insufficient progress refers to lack of progress over time. Scientific, research-based intervention refers to instructional methods such as those used with RTI. Mason's and Noah's charts in chapter 2 are examples of progress monitoring in reading fluency over time. We'll discuss progress monitoring further in chapter 6.

3. States may also permit school districts to use other research-based methods. Those methods should also consider progress over time using frequent testing and adjustments in instruction similar to RTI.

4. There must be evidence that your child exhibits a pattern of strengths and weaknesses in performance, achievement, or both, relative to age; State-approved grade-level standards or intellectual development that is determined by a group to be relevant to the identification of a specific learning disability.

Comment

4a. Some states or school districts interpret a pattern of strength and weaknesses to mean a severe discrepancy between intelligence and achievement. A severe discrepancy refers to a gap in scores between the results of an intelligence test and the results on an individual achievement test.

4b. Other states or districts interpret a pattern of strengths and weaknesses to mean strength and weakness in school performance and academic achievement. School performance refers information such as report card grades, teacher comments on a report card or work samples. Academic achievement refers to the results of standardized achievement tests or progress monitoring results. These options will be discussed further in chapters 7 and 8.

The reference to "a group" in this regulation refers to the IEP team.

5. The team must determine that its findings are not primarily the result of visual, hearing, motor disability, intellectual disability, emotional

disability, cultural factors, environmental or economic disadvantage, or limited English proficiency.

Comment: This requirement is referred to as exclusionary language. The team must find that none of the exclusions mentioned above is your child's primary disability. Your child may have another disability, but that disability cannot be primary.

6. Your child cannot be determined to be a child with a disability if they have not had appropriate instruction in reading and mathematics.

Comment: The meaning of the word "appropriate" is the same as scientific, research-based instruction. This means there must be objective evidence documenting your child's progress in reading and math in the regular classroom or as part of the referral process or she cannot be found eligible in the LD category. That documentation will be provided to you by your child's teacher or a special education teacher.

7. There must be an observation of your child in her classroom prior to or as part of the referral process for special education.

Comment: The observation will be completed by a member of the IEP team. It may be a counselor, school psychologist, or another teacher, depending on who will attend the meeting.

8. The team cannot use a single measure or assessment to determine your child's eligibility in the LD category.

Comment: The team must use a variety of assessments and other relevant information, including input from you and your child's teacher.

Although it's not an IDEA requirement, some states also require evidence of a processing disorder for your child to be eligible for special education in the LD category. A processing disorder refers to the way your child performs mental tasks in school. Difficulty performing these mental tasks is believed to point to the underlying cause of a learning disability. Testing for a processing disorder is typically completed by a school psychologist. You can find out if it's a requirement in your district by calling your district's special education office or your state's department of special education.

Four Types of Meetings

There are four types of meetings you can attend for your child. There is also a way you can make changes to an IEP without a meeting. It's important to understand the purpose of each.

Initial Evaluations

Your child's initial evaluation, of course, is to determine if she qualifies for special education. That evaluation is not only about how she's doing academically. If there's a reason to, the team will also look at your child's health, vision, hearing, social, or emotional functioning, general intelligence, communication, and motor abilities.

The team must also look at any other area where your child is suspected of having a disability. Some states require a screening or evaluation in a number of these areas as part of an initial evaluation. A screening provides a general sense of how your child performs in a skill area. It's used to determine if more thorough testing (an evaluation) is needed.

Annual Reviews

An annual review occurs each year after your child has an IEP. It's used to

- review your child's progress toward meeting the goals in her IEP;
- decide if goals should be removed because they have been mastered, or if new ones should be added;
- decide if your child's special education services—such as the amount time she receives services or the size of her group—needs to be changed; and

- decide if related services, such as speech or services for motor functioning, should be changed.

If a team believes your child's skills have reached grade level (standardized test scores at or above 90, 25, and 8 discussed in chapter 2), they must conduct a full evaluation before they can drop her from special education.

Re-evaluations

A re-evaluation (also called a triennial evaluation) occurs every three years. Some or all of the original assessments for your child may be completed as a part of a re-evaluation. It's also used to determine if your child will continue to be eligible for special education.

A re-evaluation is the most likely time a team will consider dropping your child from special education because this is when a team is expected to complete a full evaluation. However, if your child is doing well, you can decide with the school district to have fewer tests completed.

You can even decide that a re-evaluation is not necessary and instead have an annual review meeting. The IEP team will meet before an initial or re-evaluation meeting to decide if they have enough information to hold a meeting without new testing or other relevant information. If they believe they have enough information, they must inform you and explain the reason for their decision.

Your district is not required to do new testing unless you request it. If, on the other hand, the team believes new testing is required for a re-evaluation, you'll receive a form with a list of the tests they believe will be needed. You'll need to give your written approval for the district to proceed. If you believe your child will need additional testing, there will be space on the form to make that request. As long as the team agrees with your request, they will complete that testing.

Your district may decide to change its eligibility requirements between the time of your child's initial evaluation and a re-evaluation. If they do, they will let you know what testing will be appropriate using its new requirements.

Additional Meetings

Meetings can be held at other times as well if you have special concerns. For example, if you see that your child is doing poorly in a skill area, you don't need to wait until an annual review to resolve it. It's best to ask for an informal meeting with the special education teacher first, to see if you can find a solution. However, you don't need to do that. You can ask for a meeting with the IEP team at any time. That meeting must be agreed to by your district.

You can also agree to amend (change) part of the IEP without a meeting. An amendment doesn't take the place of an annual review meeting. It's used if you want to make a change between one annual review and the next. When the district writes an amendment, the changes will become part of your child's IEP. The district must send a copy of the changes to all team members, and they will also send you a copy of the changes.

If you would like more information on initial IEP meetings or re-evaluations, you'll find the following link helpful http://www.parentcenterhub.org/repository/partb-subpartd/

Putting It All Together

Figure 3.1 is another way you can understand how federal and state regulations apply to your district. All districts must use list items 1, 5, 6, 7, and 8 (above) for initial evaluations and re-evaluations. In addition, districts will select one or more of the options below to determine your child's eligibility.

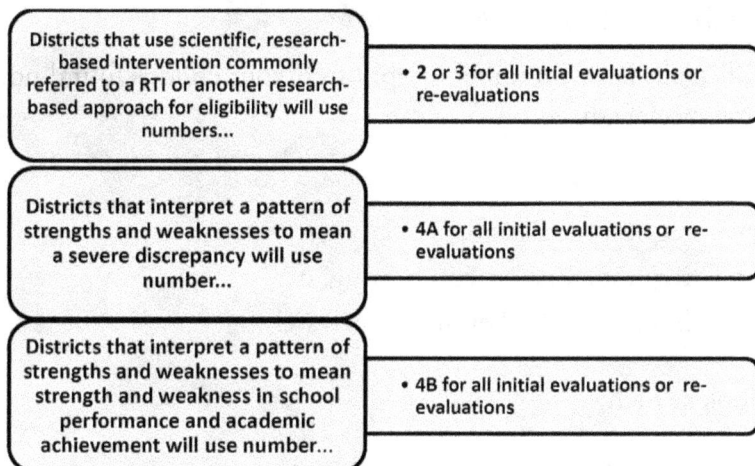

Districts that use scientific, research-based intervention commonly referred to a RTI or another research-based approach for eligibility will use numbers...	• 2 or 3 for all initial evaluations or re-evaluations
Districts that interpret a pattern of strengths and weaknesses to mean a severe discrepancy will use number...	• 4A for all initial evaluations or re-evaluations
Districts that interpret a pattern of strengths and weaknesses to mean strength and weakness in school performance and academic achievement will use number...	• 4B for all initial evaluations or re-evaluations

Figure 3.1. Learning disability eligibility options used by school districts

What all of this means is that you'll need to be aware which of options— 2, 3, 4a, or 4b— will be used for your child's initial evaluation or re-evaluation. You can find this out by calling the special education office in your district if this is your child's initial evaluation, or your child's special education teacher if it's for a re-evaluation. You'll learn much more about each of the options in chapters 6, 7, and 8.

When a Request Is Denied

Although it's rare, sometimes a district will deny a request for an initial evaluation. This will happen if they believe your child doesn't need special education. The district must inform you in writing and state the reason for their refusal. They must also send you a copy of your rights, including your right to request a due process hearing (more below).

You have other options, as well. You can decide to

- wait while you collect more information and then resubmit your request for an initial evaluation, or
- have your child evaluated privately and then resubmit your request for an initial evaluation.

We'll discuss these options further in chapter 4.

When Your Child Is Not Eligible

You will again have a number of options if your child is found not eligible for special education. You can

- request an IEE,
- request mediation,
- request a due process hearing, or
- have your child evaluated privately.

Let's look at each.

Independent Educational Evaluation

An IEE is an evaluation completed by a professional who is not associated with the school district. It's used when you disagree with the school district's testing. The IEE will be paid for by the school district.

The district will send you a letter stating its findings from the initial evaluation and a copy of your rights. The district's letter should be accompanied by a list of its requirements for IEEs as well as a list of independent evaluators it recommends. You don't have to use the professionals on that list although you should seriously consider them before you consider another professional. It's best for you to make your request for an IEE in writing. You don't have to explain why you're requesting the IEE but it's reasonable to do so. You can use sample letter 3 in appendix I as a guide.

The district may deny your request for an IEE. If they do, they must initiate a due process hearing (more below) to show that their evaluations were appropriate. As with an initial evaluation, districts rarely deny a request for an IEE.

Mediation

Mediation can also be considered if your child is found not eligible for special education. However, requesting an IEE is a more appropriate first step if your child is found not eligible and you disagree with the district's findings. The IEE may provide fresh evidence that will support your child's eligibility.

I recommend using mediation after your child has an IEP. For example, you may have a disagreement with the school district over the number of minutes per week your child will receive a service. If you're close to an agreement and you believe it can be resolved using someone who is impartial, you should consider mediation.

Mediators are professionals trained to work with parents and school districts to find solutions to disputes such as the one in our example. Mediation typically requires compromise so you will consider mediation if you're prepared to give up something in return for getting some of what you want. There is no cost for mediation.

Due Process Hearing

If you believe you will be unable to reach an agreement or if you simply prefer to, you can bypass mediation and go directly to a due process hearing. If you're going to request a due process hearing over a finding that your child is not eligible for special education, I recommend again waiting until after you have had an IEE (you may also elect to have your child evaluated privately at your expense in place of an IEE).

If the school district finds your child is still not eligible after reviewing an IEE or private evaluation, that is the best time to consider requesting a due process hearing. You can also use a due process hearing in disputes over your child's placement—such as a placement in a LD day school, for example.

A due process hearing is structured like a court hearing, where both sides present evidence and may call witnesses to testify. A hearing officer presides over the hearing (similar to a judge) and is free to ask questions, reject information, or request additional information. It's the hearing officer who will make a final decision about your child's placement and/or services. Their decision is binding on both parties unless you or the school district decides to challenge a hearing decision in a district court.

You may hire an advocate or a special education attorney for mediation. I recommend hiring a special education attorney for a hearing. You'll be required to pay the full cost of a hearing. In some cases, you may be able to recover all or part of your costs for a hearing if you prevail (win) or you partially prevail.

Filing a Complaint

Another option you have to resolve disputes is to use your state's complaint resolution procedure. Each state has a division to review complaints by parents regarding special education issues.

The usual reason to file a complaint is if your district is not providing the services stated in your child's IEP. There's a procedure you must follow if you want to file a complaint. You can speak to someone at your state department of special education to find out more. It's a good idea to ask someone knowledgeable about your state's procedures to review your complaint before you submit it. An advocate is a good choice.

Once you have filed a complaint, someone from your state department will very likely contact you to discuss it before taking their next steps. The state will investigate the complaint and send you and the school district a written notice of its decision. If the school district is found to be in violation, they will typically be required to make up the lost services either during the school year or during the summer. There is no cost to file a complaint.

Key Concepts

To understand how a team will decide on your child's eligibility, the meetings you will attend once your child has an IEP, and how to resolve conflicts, you will need to

- know the eight IDEA requirements all states and school districts must use to determine eligibility in the LD category;

- know the additional requirement some states use to determine eligibility;
- know the four types of meetings you will attend and their purpose, as well as how to change your child's IEP without a meeting; and
- understand your options if your district denies a referral for an evaluation, finds your child not eligible for special education, or is not implementing your child's IEP according to your state's regulations.

Stress Check

You learned in this chapter that you can use the law to get needed services for your child if your district isn't providing them. You should not feel uncomfortable about doing that. Remember that there's a lot at stake for your child. Her skills need to be as close to grade level as possible to support her belief in success. That won't happen unless she has intensive services as early as possible.

IEEs, mediation, and filing a complaint are designed for you and the school district to come to an agreement. And there's no cost to you. A due process hearing will be at your expense but you will only use it in situations where you know there's a critical need for a change (see chapter 11 for more information).

Your responsibility when you're using any of the remedies above is to make sure you have collected the proper information and used the support of an advocate, attorney, or knowledgeable friend before you make a request for a change (see chapters 4 and 5 for more information). It will help to reduce any stress you may have about your meeting.

Chapter 4
Collecting Information to Use at Team Meetings

Gathering information from multiple sources is essential if you want to make a persuasive case for eligibility, increased services, or a change of placement.

This chapter continues our discussion of the foundation knowledge needed to improve your skills and be your child's best advocate. If you're new to special education, the amount of information you can collect about your child may seem overwhelming at first.

Realize, however, that much of the information discussed will be mailed to you or shared at parent–teacher conferences. You won't have to spend a lot of time tracking down information. It will be more a matter of organizing the information you receive so you can use it effectively. And there will be plenty of suggestions to help you to do that as you read this and the coming chapters.

If your child already has an IEP, you can view this chapter as a test of your knowledge. Is there information that you haven't been collecting that you can use to support your requests for more services or a change of placement? Remember that the more relevant information you collect, the stronger your case will be when you make a request.

Why You Should Collect Information

It's important to collect information for the following reasons:

- If you're considering special education, you'll need test results and other relevant information to help you decide if you should refer your child for an evaluation. In other words, you'll want information that will confirm what your gut is telling you.

- You'll also want to collect information because you can use it to support your child's eligibility for special education (or continuing special education if this is a re-evaluation).

- Once your child has an IEP, collecting information will allow you to know if he's making adequate progress each year (see Closing the Gap in Skills in chapter 2 for more).

- It's also very likely that you'll want to request more services once your child has an IEP, or you may even want to request a change of placement. When that happens, the information you collect will place you in the strongest possible position to have your request approved.

As you collect information, you'll also need to consider whether a private evaluation or a school district evaluation is more appropriate for your child. And you'll be thinking about when to refer your child for an evaluation as well as how to refer him. We'll discuss each of these in this chapter as well.

The Need for Objective and Subjective Information

Table 4.1 is a list of tests and other relevant information you can gather about your child. The left column is made up of tests and reports that provide objective information. The right column is made up of tests and reports that will be considered subjective by an IEP team. That doesn't mean that subjective information should be dismissed, however. It will provide supporting evidence about whether your child is mastering skills.

Although subjective, reports by a teacher and by you or as a result of a classroom observation are also valuable because they will describe how your child copes on a day-to-day basis in school and at home. The combination of objective and subjective information will give you and the team a comprehensive picture of your child's progress and the impact his behavior is having on his learning.

Table 4.1 Objective and subjective information used at team meetings	
Objective information	Subjective information
Standardized tests by special education	Criterion-referenced testing by special education teachers
Progress monitoring	Criterion-referenced testing by classroom teachers
Work samples	Teacher's comments on a report card
Private standardized testing	Teacher's Verbal Comments
District testing*	Report card grades
State Testing*	An observation of your child in school
Reports on functional skills**	Your observations of your child at home
Testing for a processing disorder ***	Your Child's and Family's History

*Considered less dependable because they are given in a group setting

**Reports on functional skills, such as testing for speech, language skills, or motor skills, will be objective. They can also be subjective, such as a report on your child's progress in counseling.

***Testing for a processing disorder is no longer required in some states.

Objective Measures

The following objective measures are important because they will provide factual information about your child's progress. They're an essential component of a comprehensive evaluation.

Standardized Tests

Standardized tests are important because they give reliable and valid results and they will allow you to compare your child to peers at the same age and grade level. You may recall from chapter 2 that you can also use the standard scores from standardized tests to tell if your child is falling behind his peers (is regressing).

Standardized tests are widely available at all grade levels and are used for many areas of special education. For example, you'll have objective information available in areas such as reading, writing, spelling, math, speech, and language, as well as large and fine motor skills.

Progress Monitoring

You may recall from chapter 2 as well that progress monitoring is the testing component of RTI. It may also be called CBM. RTI is not used in all districts, but you'll have the option of using it if it's offered (more on RTI in chapter 6).

Progress monitoring reports use graphs that are easy to understand. Tests are available to assess your child weekly, allowing his teacher to monitor his growth in skills and to make changes in instruction. If he's not making progress, changes usually occur every eight weeks.

Another advantage of progress monitoring, is that each test your child receives will test his understanding of grade level skills for a whole school year. This means that as he progresses through the year, the teacher will know if he's remembering skills taught earlier.

Work Samples

Work samples are valuable because they provide a picture of your child's progress in skill areas such as writing, spelling, and math.

You can also receive objective information in reading in the early grades (first and second grade) by asking your child's teacher for samples of his oral reading. Teachers in these grades test students frequently using short stories or word lists that are samples of text at your child's grade level.

The samples will clearly show your child's reading progress. These "tests" are referred to as running records or informal reading inventories. If running records or informal inventories are not used in grade three and beyond, tape recording your child reading is an excellent way to document his reading skills. This should be completed close to the time of your child's evaluation meeting.

Your child's teacher can provide grade level books if you need them. Your recording, including copies of the reading passage used and which shows your child's errors, will provide a reliable sample of your child's reading skills for team members to review.

Private Testing

Private testing is an option you may choose if you would like to compare your child's skills or behavior to your school district's testing. Private testing will be comprehensive and will typically assess your child's basic skills, intelligence, social, and emotional growth, speech, language, and motor skills, as well as evidence of a processing disorder, which evaluates how your child responds to specific mental tasks encountered in school and in other settings. Where difficulties are found, they're believed to point to the presence of a learning disability. Private testing can be helpful if there's a dispute over your child's services or placement. It can also be used to provide information that will support your child's initial evaluation or re-evaluation.

District Testing

District tests (if they are given) are another useful measure of your child's skill levels. Typically they will test all basic skills—reading, writing, spelling, and math—comparing your child to others at his age and grade level.

District tests are also standardized, providing reliable and valid information about your child's progress. However, they're considered less dependable because they're given in a group setting. When you're reviewing all of your child's information, you should give a higher priority to special education or private testing because they will be individually administered tests.

State Testing

State tests are required as a result of federal legislation called No Child Left Behind (NCLB) and are given in all school districts in reading and math in grades three through eight and once in high school. They're also given in science, once each at the elementary, middle, and high school levels. State tests also use standardized procedures and the results can be considered reliable and valid. About one-half of the states require all children to pass a state test to graduate from high school. If your child has an IEP and your state requires students to pass a state test for graduation, it will apply to your child as well. Note: many states add requirements to those listed above.

One of the important things you'll need to do is to make sure your child has appropriate accommodations in his IEP. Accommodations are changes that are made that don't alter what a test measures. For example, if your child requires a quiet environment to take a test or he must use a word processor because of motor difficulties, they're referred to as accommodations. .

Your child should be able to use most of his accommodations on a state test. There will be some exceptions, however, and the IEP team will know what they are. To find out more about accommodations, you'll find the following link helpful: http://www.parentcenterhub. org/repository/accommodations/

Reports on Functional Skills

Functional skills are skills such as behavior, social skills, motor skills, or communication (speech and language) skills. The goals and objectives for these areas will be written by the professional who provides your child's services. They should also provide objective information about your child's progress wherever possible.

Behavior here refers to behaviors such as attention deficit hyperactivity disorder (ADHD), attention deficit disorder (ADD), and emotional needs such as anxiety or depression. You can receive objective information in areas such as motor or communication skills, but you may not in areas such as ADHD, ADD, social skills, or counseling. You will, however, receive regular progress reports in all of these important areas from the professional providing your child's services, just as you would for an academic skill.

It's important to give the same consideration to your child's functional skill improvement as you would to academic skills. That's because a functional skill can have a direct impact on academic functioning. For example, if your child is receiving counseling services for anxiety, his anxiety can affect his progress in all skill areas. As your child's anxiety diminishes, you should observe if there is a corresponding improvement in his grades. Other functional skills for the child with LD, such as behavior or difficulty with social, motor, or communication skills, can have a similar impact.

Testing for a Processing Disorder

As I mentioned earlier, a diagnosis of a processing disorder is thought by many professionals to provide evidence of the underlying cause of your child's learning disability. Of course, that diagnosis alone will not qualify your child for special education in the LD category. It must be supported by evidence of weak skills found in achievement testing and/or lack of progress learning skills over time (RTI) along with other relevant information.

Some states no longer require evidence of a processing disorder. You can find out if evidence of a processing disorder is used in your district by calling your district's special education office. If you have your child tested privately, it's important let the evaluator know if identification of a processing disorder is required by your district.

Subjective Measures

The reports on the right side of table 4.1 will be considered subjective by the IEP team. Although not factual, subjective measures do provide useful information about your child's behavior in and outside of school and will support the findings from objective tests. Let's look more closely at this important dimension of testing.

Criterion-Referenced Testing

You recall from chapter 2 that criterion-referenced tests are the quizzes or tests given by a teacher that later become your child's grades on his report card or progress reports written by a special education teacher. You may also recall that these tests are frequently not standardized—the tests will have unknown reliability or validity. When you're reviewing your child's testing, you should give a higher priority to any tests on the left side of table 5.1.

Teacher's Comments and Report Cards

Your child's report card, the teacher's comments on a report card, and the teacher's comments at a parent–teacher conference or an IEP meeting will also be considered subjective. Report card grades or comments related to those grades should not be used unless they're realistic.

A realistic grade is one in which the teacher uses the same method of scoring for your child as for all students. Sometimes in the early grades a teacher will change the method of scoring and assign a higher grade to encourage your child. That's commendable, but those grades should not be used at an IEP meeting. They'll give an unrealistic picture of your child's progress.

An Observation of Your Child in School

For an initial evaluation or re-evaluation that may be also called a triennial (three year) evaluation, the district must complete an observation of your child in his classroom. The observation will focus on your child's skills and behavior that may affect his learning. The results will be reported at your child's IEP meeting. Notice that an observation is not required for the years between an initial and a triennial evaluation.

Your Observations of Your Child at Home

You should also be prepared to discuss your child's behavior if you know he's stressed as a result of his belief that he can't perform in a subject. Keep a record of any of the following signs of stress:

- Negative comments that are repeated frequently such as "I'm dumb," "I'm stupid," "I don't get it," "it's too hard," "I can't do it," "the homework is stupid," "the teachers are stupid," "I'm not going to school," or "I'm feeling sick" when you know he is not sick.

- Negative behaviors (especially in middle and high school) such as forgetting his homework, losing his homework, avoiding long term projects until the last minute, not studying for tests, not asking for help, or not going for help when it's offered.

These behaviors, which I discussed in chapter 1, are signs that your child is discouraged and believes he can't be successful. If a behavior (such as anxiety or acting out) is present in school and it's affecting your child's progress, you'll need to request counseling or a behavior management program to address it. You can learn more about behavior management programs from your district's school psychologist.

Your Child's and Your Family's History

Your family's history will provide important information to the team regarding your child's LD. Keep a record of your child's developmental milestones. They include areas such as when your child began to walk and talk, whether there were significant childhood illnesses or ear infections, and whether speech and/or motor skills were delayed. If other members of your immediate or extended family have a history of LD, it's important to share that information if you're able to as well.

You'll also want to keep a record of difficulties your child may have had in preschool or kindergarten in any of the following skills:

- fine and/or large motor skills
- speech and language skills
- social skills
- remembering dates, phone numbers, and addresses
- learning how to rhyme words
- learning the alphabet

School District and Private Evaluations

You'll want to consider whether a school district or private evaluation is best for your child as you gather information as well. Let's look at the strengths and weaknesses of each:

School District Evaluations

Strengths

A school district will

- know how your child has progressed over time. If progress monitoring is used, it will bring objectivity to reports about your child's progress over time.
- use information from multiple sources that document your child's progress, such as standardized achievement testing, district testing, state testing, work samples, report cards, criterion-referenced testing, and teacher's comments.
- complete its evaluation in a relatively short period of time (6 to 12 weeks).
- complete its evaluation at no cost to you.

Weaknesses

A school district will

- typically not have professionals to complete in-depth testing in areas such as neurological or emotional/behavioral functioning. The school district will pay for an additional evaluation(s) if it's recommended. However, it may delay a decision on eligibility or delay a service until the evaluation is completed.
- only test your child in a particular area if they have evidence of a weakness. This means there may be some areas that you believe should be tested that will not be because the school lacks evidence to support your request.

Private Evaluations

Strengths

A private evaluation will

- be comprehensive and will include tests of your child's achievement, intelligence, social growth, speech and language skills, motor skills, and testing for a processing disorder.
- typically include in-depth neurological or emotional/ behavioral testing. This means that this additional testing can be completed at the time your child is evaluated.

Weaknesses

A private evaluation will

- usually take six to nine months to complete, which will delay the start of services for your child if this is an initial evaluation.
- typically not be able to determine your child's response to instruction over time, and
- be at your expense.

The bottom line is that a decision on a school district or private testing is personal. Keep in mind that if you choose a school district evaluation and you're not satisfied with the results, you can request an IEE. (See chapter 3 for more on independent evaluations.)

When Should You Refer Your Child?

Your ideal time to refer your child is the middle of first grade or as soon after that as possible. You recall from chapter 1 that in addition to your genuine belief in your child's success, you want to start intensive services in first or second grade to prevent your child from forming a negative belief about his skills and abilities.

If your child is in third grade or beyond, you should refer him immediately. At this level, you may have to sacrifice some of the information you would collect in order to start the referral process. You will do that in addition to carrying your belief in your child's success, to try to minimize the impact that a belief may have on his performance.

Even if your child is in third grade or beyond, however, you can collect information during the time he's being evaluated for special education. That's typically a six to twelve-week period. You'll also want to pull together any information you may have collected in earlier grades. This information may include progress monitoring, work samples, district testing, state testing, functional skill reports, report card grades and comments, as well as your observations of your child at home.

You'll want to collect as much information as you can from the list in table 4.1. Remember that you'll be able to request work samples from kindergarten forward, and you'll receive state testing starting in third grade. Also, the results of progress monitoring and district testing will be mailed to you or reported to you at parent–teacher conferences as long as they're offered by your district. Of course, you'll receive report cards three or four times a year as well.

If your child is in first grade, I recommend that you collect information until February and then make a referral. Collect information in second grade until your child's first report card (about November) as well as any information you may have from kindergarten and first grade, and then refer your child. For other grades, refer your child immediately (see above discussion for third grade and beyond).

How Do You Refer Your Child?

You should make a referral in writing to the director of special education in your district. You can use sample letter 1 in appendix I as a guide if you're requesting a school district evaluation. Use sample letter 2 in appendix I as a guide if you have had your child evaluated privately.

Key Concepts

To understand what information you will collect about your child, you will need to

- know what objective and subjective information you can collect;
- know the purpose of each kind of information;
- understand the differences between school district and private evaluations; and
- know when and how to request an evaluation.

Stress Check

Collecting information is so important because it provides a way for you to support your requests for your child. If you haven't collected information, it will be a wise choice to have your child tested privately before you make a request.

Objective information is necessary but also keep in mind that subjective information such as a teacher's comments, an observation of your child in school, your observation of your child at home, and your family's history will provide important supporting evidence for your requests as well.

A dilemma in special education is that a team is most likely to respond to your request for a change if you have strong objective evidence supported by other relevant information. Yet the school district is not likely to use objective testing after an initial evaluation up until the time of a re-evaluation.

That doesn't mean your only option is to have your child tested privately. In chapter 9, I'll show you a way to request objective information each year that will give you the information you need and won't be time consuming for a special education teacher.

Your goal, is to walk into your meeting with strong evidence to support your requests for change. When you have taken the time do that, by collecting evidence, or through a private evaluation, and you have proper support (see chapter 5), you'll feel relaxed and confident about the outcome of your meeting.

Chapter 5
Finding Proper Support

Proper support is crucial as you move thorough the special education process. To be in the strongest possible position to have your requests approved, you will need to know when an expert is required.

In this foundation chapter, we'll take a close look at the training and skills needed by an advocate or attorney for you to feel properly supported for the type of meeting you will attend. That doesn't mean you'll need someone with you at all your meetings.

The purpose of *Becoming Your Child's Best Advocate* is to empower you so you'll feel confident and comfortable attending meetings on your own. When you first decide to attend a meeting without and advocate or attorney, you may want a friend to attend with you. As you gain experience and realize that you have the knowledge and necessary skills, you'll find that a friend may no longer be needed.

There are certain types of meetings, however, where it will be a wise choice to use an advocate or attorney. Those meetings are

- initial evaluations;
- re-evaluations, if the team will consider dropping your child;
- the first time you make a request to increase your child's services;
- when requesting a placement in an LD self-contained program in your district; and
- when requesting a placement in an LD day school.

There are critical decisions to make in each type of meeting and we'll cover them in detail in the coming chapters. Here, however, we'll look at identifying the proper professional for the type of meeting you will attend.

Initial Evaluations

Table 5.1 shows the types of meetings in which it will be important to have an advocate or attorney. Initial evaluations (category 1) will require an advocate who is skilled at interpreting achievement test results and knows the four methods of determining eligibility—RTI, other research-based approaches, a severe discrepancy method, and a pattern of strengths and weaknesses (see chapter 3 for more).

That advocate should also be knowledgeable about all parts of the IEP, but be particularly skilled at

- knowing your child's present level of performance (PLOP) from test data and other relevant information. PLOP refers to what your child can do now in a skill area.
- writing measurable goals and objectives. A measurable goal or objective is one that is written with a number or percent of correct responses such as earning a score of 7 out of 10 on a spelling test or 85 percent on a math test.
- knowing the kind and amount of services your child will require to meet her needs.

These are the essential elements of the IEP.

Use the following link if you would like to find out more about IEPs.

http://www.parentcenterhub.org/repository/iep/

The links below will give you an idea of how goals and objectives are designed and what well written goals and objectives look like.

http://www.p12.nysed.gov/specialed/publications/iepguidance/annual.htm
http://www.attainmentcompany.com/sites/default/files/pdf/sample/WMIEP_Sample.pdf

Table 5.1 Qualifications and skills needed for different types of meetings			
	Type of meeting	Qualifications	Skills
1	Requesting an initial evaluation or re-evaluation from a school district	Special education supervisor Special education advocate	Highly skilled at writing IEPs Understands how a team will determine eligibility using RTI, a severe discrepancy method, or a pattern of strengths and weaknesses Skilled at interpreting achievement test results
2	Requesting an initial evaluation or re-evaluation from a private evaluator	School/clinical or neuropsychologist	Highly skilled at administering and interpreting tests Understands how a team will determine eligibility using RtI, a severe discrepancy method, or a pattern of strengths and weaknesses Understands the team meeting process
3	Requesting an increase in services	Special education supervisor Speech therapist Special education advocate	Experience working in (or understands) all basic skill areas Highly skilled in (or understands) research-based instruction Skilled at interpreting test results Skilled at observing a program to determine if it's meeting your child's needs
4	Requesting a placement in an LD self-contained program		
5	Requesting an LD Day Placement	A Special education attorney Special education supervisor* Special education advocate*	Experience representing parents in disputes over placements Skilled in special education law
		B School/clinical or neuropsychologist	Highly skilled at administering and interpreting tests
		C Special education supervisor Special education advocate	Skilled at observing a program to determine if it will meet your child's needs

* A special education supervisor or special education advocate (5A) will need to have experience representing parents in disputes over placements and to be knowledgeable about special education law. Notice that they can be used in 5C separately or in combination with 5A.

Re-evaluations

I recommend using one of the advocates in category 1 in the table above for a re-evaluation. One purpose of a re-evaluation is to determine if your child is still eligible for special education. You'll need to be prepared if the team recommends dropping your child. You can use the information in appendix II as a guide to review with your advocate before your meeting. The team must complete a full evaluation if they anticipate dropping your child from services.

If your district is not intending to drop your child, you should not need to use an advocate for your re-evaluation meeting. The team may send you a notice that they believe they have enough current information to make a decision about your child's continued eligibility. You should request updated standardized achievement testing in basic skills as well as for a related service, such as speech or motor skills. You can request other testing as well. Remember that if you don't request updated testing, the district is not obliged to do it.

Whatever additional objective or subjective information you have collected about your child can be used by you and your advocate to support your child's continued eligibility for special education.

Private Evaluations

You will use category 2 if you decide to have your child evaluated privately for an initial evaluation or re-evaluation (see chapter 4 for a comparison of school district and private evaluations). It will be important to tell the evaluator whether your child's eligibility will be determined using RTI, another research-based approach, a severe discrepancy method, or a pattern of strengths and weaknesses, discussed in chapter 3. That information will determine the kind of testing they will complete and the focus of their report. The private evaluators we are discussing are highly skilled at administering and interpreting tests. Their test battery will be very thorough.

The private evaluator you use may not be an expert at writing IEPs. If that's the case, you can wait until you receive a copy of your child's

IEP. Then, use one of the advocates shown in category 1 to review it and make suggestions for changes before you sign it (you should share your child's test results with them as well). If there are major changes, use them again once you receive a revised IEP to make sure it's one that will meet your child's needs.

Requesting an Increase in Services

Notice that most of the skills needed in category 3 of table 5.1 are different than those for an initial evaluation. I recommend using one of the advocates on the list if this is the first time you're requesting an increase in services. You may be surprised that a speech therapist is on the list. Speech therapists have become much more involved in basic skill remediation—especially in the areas of reading and writing over the past 15 years.

You'll want an advocate who is skilled at interpreting achievement test results, and has experience teaching reading, writing, spelling, and math or is knowledgeable about basic skill instruction. They should also be knowledgeable about research-based instruction and skilled at observing a program to see if it's meeting your child's needs. This combination of skills will allow them to know what increase in services your child will need as well as the research-based approach and frequency of testing needed to monitor her progress. We'll discuss requesting an increase in services further in chapter 9.

Placement in an LD Self-Contained Program

Your child will receive all of her basic skills, including reading, writing, spelling, and math, if she is in a self-contained program at the elementary level. At the middle and high school levels, she may attend regular classes supported by special education staff.

The advocate you hire should be able to interpret achievement test results and have experience teaching all basic skills (or is knowledgeable about basic skill instruction) using research-based instructional materials. They're particularly valuable because they will be able to observe your district's self-contained program and determine if it will be a suitable environment for your child. We'll discuss self-contained programs in more detail in chapter 10.

Placement in an LD Day School

Your primary support for a placement in an LD day school should come from an advocate who is skilled in special education law and experienced at representing parents in disputes over placements. A special education attorney, as well as a special education supervisor or special education advocate (with the skills and experience noted above), should be your first choice for that support.

An attorney will let you know if you'll need a psychologist to test your child (5B) or an advocate (5C) to observe your child. They will also let you know if the psychologist or the person who observes your child should attend your meeting.

A special education supervisor or special education advocate will be in a dual role (5A and C) if you use them as your advocate. They will, therefore, represent you in a meeting and complete an observation if it's needed. They will also advise you if they believe your child needs to be tested by a psychologist. There is much more to discuss about LD day school programs that we will cover in chapter 11.

Where to Start your Search

For Advocates

You can start your search for an advocate using your local parents' group for children with disabilities. If you do that, I recommend speaking to at least three parents about a professional recommended by them so you have a good sense of their skills and their personal style.

You can also investigate private tutoring services in your area. A special education supervisor or speech therapist in private practice may work in a group practice in your district. You can ask if they advocate for parents.

The advocates named above can also be found at local or regional hospital clinics or at universities that offer evaluation and tutoring services to children and adolescents. The professional who will work directly with parents will most likely be called an educational liaison.

Many advocates will be in private practice by themselves and will advertise in local newspapers or online. An important thing to know is whether they are certified, licensed or trained in advocacy and have experience working in schools. You can find that out by asking for a resume.

Although it may seem unusual, also call the director of special education or supervisor of special education in your district (they may also be called a special education coordinator, team leader, or team chairperson) and ask if the advocate you have chosen has attended meetings in your district. Ask their opinion of that advocate.

If they advise you to use someone else, weigh what they say carefully. They will know who is knowledgeable and who is particularly positive (or negative) in their approach at IEP meetings. They will very likely be able to give you names of other advocates to consider as well.

For Attorneys

To get a preliminary list of attorneys, call your school district's special education office and ask for the name of the special education attorney they use. Keep in mind that you can't use that attorney because that would create a conflict of interest.

Then call the special education offices of five or six communities surrounding your area, and ask for the names of the special education attorneys they use. Don't be surprised if the special education attorney your district uses works for some of those districts as well. However, you should end up with the names of three or four attorneys. Many attorneys will represent parents in communities where they do not work for a school district.

Why do I recommend calling school districts? The attorneys hired by school districts will be highly qualified and experienced special education attorneys. That's the kind of professional you want to represent you. You can check with your local parents' group for children with disabilities as well to learn more about the personal style of the attorneys on your list.

You can also use the following links if you're not successful using the approaches described above:

http://www.advocatesforspecialeducation.com/find.htm

http://www.yellowpagesforkids.com/

Financial Considerations

Parents from your local parents' group for children with disabilities can also share the names of advocates who will work on a sliding fee scale (at a rate based on your income) or attorneys who work pro bono (offer free services to low income clients). When you have identified several professionals, call their service to confirm that they offer adjusted rates.

Training and Experience

The following is a list of the essential skills I recommend for an advocate or attorney. You can look for those skills on a resume:

Look for an advocate who

- has worked in public schools or an LD day school;
- has worked extensively with the LD population;
- is certified or licensed or has been trained as a special education advocate; and
- has a minimum of three years of experience representing parents as an advocate.

Look for an attorney who

- works full time as special education attorney;
- has a minimum of three years of experience representing parents in special education matters; and
- has worked extensively with the LD population.

The link below will give you more information and questions you can ask an advocate or attorney regarding their training and experience:

http://advocatesforspecialeducation.com/guidelines.html

You should interview the professional you intend to use before you make a decision to use them. Send information to them about your child in advance and expect to pay for that visit. Also ask them to send you a resume in advance of your meeting.

After your meeting you can use table 5.2 to help you decide if you have the found the right match.

Table 5.2 Checklist to determine if an advocate or attorney is a good match			
Instructions: Ask the following questions after your meeting with an advocate or attorney. The more often you answer yes, the more certain you will feel that you have the right match.	YES	NO	Comment
Did the advocate or attorney review the information you sent in advance of your meeting?			
Were they organized in their approach?			
Did they demonstrate that they knew your child's issues and were comfortable dealing with them?			
Could they explain information so you could easily understand it?			
Did they have a planned approach for your meeting that they shared with you?			
Did they listen to your questions and did you feel reassured with their response?			
Were they easy to talk with?			
Did you feel confident in their skills?			
Did the advocate or attorney invite you to present information at the meeting?			
Were you comfortable with their personal style?			
Overall would you give them a rating of 9 or 10 out of 10?			

Key Concepts

To know which meeting will require support and that you have selected the right professional, you will need to know

- the essential meetings you should attend where an advocate or attorney will be a wise choice;
- the qualifications and skills needed for the type of meeting you will attend;
- where you will find an advocate or attorney; and
- how to decide if an advocate or attorney is the right match for you.

Stress Check

It's nice to know that one of the things you'll do—finding an advocate or attorney—is not likely to cause stress. You'll need to be thorough, however, to make sure you have a professional who is knowledgeable and experienced for the type of meeting you will attend. And you need to make sure you have someone who is compatible.

It will be reassuring to have someone with you who "knows their stuff." Your responsibility will be to gather appropriate information for your meetings (referred to in chapter 4) and to work with the advocate or attorney as a partner to find the best solution for your child's program or services.

In the remaining chapters, you'll learn how to apply your foundation skills to the type of meeting you'll attend.

Chapter 6
Attending a Meeting Where
RTI is Used

If you were to choose a criterion-reference measure of your child's progress, you would want to use progress monitoring because it will give you objective results.

You were introduced to the federal special education regulations in chapter 3. You may recall that states or school districts must select from one or more of four options and follow the additional requirements to determine your child's eligibility for special education in the LD category. You also learned that you should find out which of the methods of determining eligibility—RTI, another research-based approach, a severe discrepancy, or a pattern of strengths and weaknesses—will be used for your child's initial or re-evaluation meeting.

We'll discuss those methods in the next three chapters.

Because there's repetition of content in the next three chapters, chapter 6 will be covered in detail. You can then refer to it when you read chapters 7 and 8 if you need to review information.

Alternatively, read chapter 6 and then chapter 7 or 8 depending on which one will be used for your child's initial evaluation or re-evaluation. However, I recommend reading the chapters in sequence to understand how the methods are used to determine eligibility.

In this chapter, we'll look at a scientific research-based intervention commonly referred to as RTI. It may also be called curriculum-based assessment (CBA). Your district may use another research-based intervention. If that's the case, that method should use the same approach as RTI.

What is RTI?

RTI is a procedure that's used to identify children, usually in the early grades (it can be used at any grade level), who are at risk of failure. The identified children receive research-based instruction and their progress is monitored frequently. You'll recall that is called progress monitoring or curriculum-based measurement (CBM).

Keep in mind as you read this chapter that RTI is used in regular education and focuses on providing intensive instruction through the classroom curriculum. RTI is voluntary for your district unless your state requires it. There is no IDEA requirement for special education to use RTI.

RTI is organized in levels, and services become more intense as children progress through each level. Most districts have three levels of instruction called primary, secondary, and tertiary. Some districts may use the terms tier I, II, or III to describe their levels.

You'll be informed about RTI if your child reaches the secondary level. IDEA requires your school district to give you information about their policies regarding RTI, the data that will be collected about your child, the regular education services that will be provided, and the strategies for increasing your child's rate of learning.

It's important to understand that you can refer your child for a special education evaluation during the time they're receiving RTI. However, I recommend allowing a minimum of six weeks (eight is better) so you have enough information (data) to know whether your child is making adequate progress (more below).

If your child closes the gap in skills at any level, he will return to receive his instruction with the rest of his class. Children who are not making progress will be referred to the next level, where they will receive more intense instruction.

If a child doesn't make adequate progress at the highest level, he will very likely be recommended for a special education evaluation.

Advantages and Disadvantages of RTI

Advantages

One advantage of using RTI is that your child will receive immediate help through regular education in the early grades. That help will become progressively more intense. If he doesn't make adequate progress, he will be referred for a special education evaluation.

The intensive help your child receives will occur in a relatively short period of time—between 6 and 36 weeks. That help will provide objective information right from day one. It will assist you in making decisions even if you stop RTI and refer your child for a special education evaluation before he reaches the highest level of service.

It's also highly likely that your child will be found eligible for special education if he has gone through all of the levels, has not made adequate progress, and his lack of progress is supported by other evaluations and relevant information. That's because one of the key symptoms used to identify a child with LD is lack of progress over time.

Disadvantages

A disadvantage of RTI is that it may not be used by your district, or if it is, it may not be used at your child's grade level. There is also no uniform standard (criterion) to determine what the term insufficient (poor) progress used in IDEA means. Each state or school district establishes its own standard.

Progress monitoring can be valuable as long as it's used with fidelity (the way it's intended). It requires support from multiple professionals to be effective and requires staff training and the purchase of materials. This can be a problem for districts with limited resources. There must also be a strong commitment by regular education to use RTI to improve student learning.

Each district also determines how many students it will service. For example, a district may decide to provide help to students with test scores in the lowest 10 percent of a class. If your district identifies 15 percent of its students who need help, the additional students may not receive RTI.

Attending a Meeting Where RTI Is Used

In chapter 5, I strongly recommend using an advocate or private evaluator who's familiar with RTI for an initial evaluation or you should use them for a re-evaluation if your district will consider dropping your child. You'll want to meet with the advocate or private evaluator before your child's evaluation and have them attend his IEP meeting with you.

The most important thing you can do to prepare for a meeting is to collect as much information as possible about your child discussed in chapter 4. That same information is presented below as well as the IDEA requirements for research-based intervention.

The Team's Priority

The team must meet the IDEA's and your state's (or district's) requirements for RTI. Those requirements are as follows (see chapter 3 for more):

1. Your child is not achieving adequately in one or more of the following areas: oral expression, listening comprehension, written expression, basic reading (phonemic awareness, phonics, vocabulary), reading fluency, reading comprehension, mathematics calculation, mathematics problem solving.

2. Your child has not made sufficient (has made poor) progress in one or more of the skills in 1, above, when using a process based on his response to scientific, research-based intervention (commonly referred to as RTI).

3. The team's findings (in 1, above) are not primarily the result of visual, hearing, motor disability, intellectual disability, cultural factors, environmental, or economic disadvantage, or limited English proficiency referred to as exclusions.*

4. Your child has had appropriate instruction in reading and mathematics.

5. There has been an observation of your child's academic performance and behavior in his area(s) of difficulty.

6. The team has used multiple measures or assessments to determine your child's eligibility in the LD category or to determine an appropriate educational program.

The above requirements apply to initial evaluations and re-evaluations.

*Some states or districts add exclusions, such as health related issues, excessive absences, and frequent change of schools, or poor motivation.

What the Team Will Pay Attention To

The team will pay particular attention to numbers 1 and 2. To determine if your child is achieving adequately, the district will typically use a standardized achievement test (1). You may recall from chapter 2 that standardized achievement testing is objective and compares your child's skills to those of his peers.

To determine your child's progress using a scientific, research-based intervention (2), the district will use progress monitoring. You may also recall that progress monitoring is the testing component of RTI. Its results are also objective. The term "insufficient progress" referred to in IDEA is also called a poor rate of progress.

When your child has low scores on a standardized achievement test and his rate of progress is insufficient (poor), professionals refer to it as a "dual discrepancy." You may also see that term used in a report.

Low achievement scores and a poor rate of progress are considered key symptoms of a child with LD. Low scores on questions 1 and poor progress on question 2, therefore, will support your child's eligibility for special education (more below).

Identify Your Child's Low Scores

When you request an evaluation for your child you will ask for the district to send you its test results two days before your team meeting (see sample letters 1 and 2 in appendix I). Wait until you receive those results before you meet with your advocate or private evaluator.

The first thing you want to do is to review your child's standardized achievement results (1) and his progress monitoring charts (2). Low achievement scores and a poor rate of progress will support your child's eligibility for special education. Look for standard scores below 90, percentiles below 25, and scaled scores below 8 when you review standardized test results (see chapter 2 for more). They are the scores that will tell you your child is going to need extra support.

You will also look for a progress monitoring profile similar to Mason's profile in chapter 2. That will tell you your child is not making sufficient progress. You won't know if your child qualifies for special education before your meeting, however, since you won't know your district's standard(s) for eligibility.

You should also review all information you have collected as well as any additional district tests you received. The following is a list of tests and other relevant information you could review in addition to numbers 1 and 2, above:

- a report of a functional skill such as speech or motor skills
- testing for a processing disorder by a school psychologist (that may be in the same report that discusses your child's IQ)
- criterion-referenced testing (tests or quizzes) by a regular or special education teacher

- district testing
- state testing
- a teacher's comments on a report card and/or report card grades
- private testing
- work samples that you collected
- your child's and family's history

You and your advocate or private evaluator will look for confirmation of the weak skills identified in 1 and/or 2, and any other weak skill(s) that may not have been identified.

Remember that confirmation of test scores from other tests and subjective information that I discussed in chapter 4 will add strength to your child's eligibility for special education.

Those scores can also become baseline information (your starting point for collecting information about your child). You can use them to compare to scores you receive each year, if he qualifies for special education, and to determine if he's closing the gap in skills (see chapter 2 for more on closing the gap in skills).

Make a List

Highlight all of your child's weak scores and comments from professionals about your child's weaknesses as you review information. I recommend making a list of those scores and comments to take to your meeting. Then you or the advocate or private evaluator can refer to them if you need to.

Send a Letter

You'll need to send a letter to your district's special education office to arrive two days in advance of the meeting informing them a professional will attend the meeting with you. You can use sample letter 4 in appendix I as a guide to write your letter.

Develop a History

Once your child has an IEP, it will be important to develop a history of his testing and other relevant information. Then you can draw on that information for a re-evaluation or to request an increase in services or a change in placement. We'll discuss requesting increased services or a change of placement in chapters 9 through 11.

Key Concepts

To understand how a team will determine your child's eligibility for special education using RTI or another research-based procedure, you will need to

- know what RTI (or another research-based procedure) is and its advantages and disadvantages;
- know what information the team will consider to determine your child's eligibility;
- know what information will support your child's eligibility for special education; and
- know what test scores and other relevant information you can take to your meeting to support your child's eligibility for special education.

Stress Check

Do you believe that RTI may be used to keep your child out of special education? If you think about the process your child will go through, you'll realize that your belief isn't justified.

It's not justified because your child will be tested weekly using standardized procedures (the results will be reliable and valid). This means the information you receive will be objective. The charts you receive of your child's progress will also show clearly what's happening.

If your child is making good progress (similar to Noah's chart in chapter 2), it means that he only needed a period of intense instruction to catch up to his peers. He will be able to return to his classroom group and receive instruction with his peers. When you add your genuine belief in your child's success that I discussed in chapter 1, you will have written a prescription for his success.

If your child is not making progress (similar to Mason's chart in chapter 2) and qualifies for special education, you and your advocate or private evaluator will know that you'll need to focus your attention on your child receiving intense services (four or five days per week).

You'll also need to monitor those services carefully to make sure your child is making adequate progress once he has an IEP. When you combine intense services with your genuine belief in your child's success, you will also have written a prescription for his success.

A third possibility is that your child's low scores (below 90, 25, and 8) on a standardized achievement test and progress monitoring supported by other information don't meet your district's standard(s) for special education eligibility. If that happens, you will want to consider one of the options discussed at the end of chapter 2. We'll discuss how you can turn those options into a prescription for success as well in chapter 7.

Your prescription for success will allow you to shift to an optimistic view whether your child is accepted into special education or not. It will help to remove your stress about the outcome of a meeting.

Chapter 7
Attending a Meeting Where a Severe Discrepancy Is Used

When the results you receive from achievement testing are unexpected compared to your child's ability, your child may have a learning disability.

You learned in chapter 6 that a team can determine your child's eligibility for special education by using scientific, research-based intervention commonly referred to as RTI or another research-based approach. You may also recall from chapter 3 that IDEA gives teams other options. In this chapter, we'll discuss the third of those options, which is called a severe discrepancy method. Note: States cannot require schools to use a severe discrepancy.

If you're reading these chapters in sequence, you'll notice the focus for chapter 7 is similar to chapter 6. This is because you will collect the same information for each type of meeting you attend. What will be different, however, is how that information will be used to determine your child's eligibility for special education. Chapter 6 considered your child's performance in basic skills over a period of time (her rate of progress).

Chapter 7 will consider your child's performance in basic skills and its relationship to an IQ test. They're different approaches to determine eligibility for special education. You'll also notice that instead of repeating information, I will refer you to chapter 6 to review any details you may need. The focus of chapter 7 will be about what's different from the basic requirements discussed in chapter 6.

What is a Severe Discrepancy Method?

A severe discrepancy is a method that looks at the correlation (relationship) between an IQ test (usually the total score) and a total or cluster score from any of the eight basic skills identified by IDEA in chapter 3.

Mathematical formulas are typically used to determine a severe discrepancy. The formulas differ in their complexity. To have a severe discrepancy, your child must meet a standard (criterion) set by your school district. That standard will vary from state to state and district to district (more below). Note: If a school district elects to use a severe discrepancy method, they may be required to use a state standard for your child's eligibility.

The idea behind a severe discrepancy is that if there is a large gap between your child's total IQ score and her achievement in one or more of the eight basic skills referred to in IDEA, it will be an unexpected result. For example, suppose your child has an IQ of 120 (in the superior range) and a standard score of 80 (in the low average range) on a test of math calculation. That's a gap of 40 points (120–80 = 40). Would you expect that to happen?

The answer is no. You would expect your child's achievement score to be close to her IQ. Professionals refer to this gap as "unexpected underachievement." It's considered a key symptom of a child with LD. Another name for unexpected underachievement is a severe discrepancy. Note: The above example is a simplification of a severe discrepancy calculation.

Advantages and Disadvantages of a Severe Discrepancy

Advantages

One advantage of a severe discrepancy is that it uses objective measures (an IQ and a standardized achievement test) to look at your child's failure to learn. Also, the most sophisticated formula used to determine a severe discrepancy is statistically sound (it will give accurate information).

Disadvantages

Like RTI, there is no uniform standard that's used to determine a severe discrepancy. States or school districts determine their own standard. Unfortunately, this means your child may qualify as LD in one state, but you may find that they do not qualify in another if you move. This difference may even be found between two districts in the same state, in those states that allow districts to determine their own standard.

Restrictions on a Severe Discrepancy

Some states no longer allow a severe discrepancy to be used in the early grades. Others do not allow a severe discrepancy at any grade level. You can find out if a severe discrepancy is used at your child's grade level from your district's special education office.

If it's not used, ask how a team will determine your child's eligibility. Your district's choices will be to use RTI or a pattern of strengths and weaknesses. I recommend reviewing the method(s) that will be used (see chapter 6 or chapter 8) before your child's IEP meeting.

Attending a Meeting Where a Severe Discrepancy Is Used

The best thing you can do to prepare for your child's meeting is to collect information from as many sources as possible discussed in chapter 4. For an initial evaluation or for a re-evaluation where the team will consider dropping your child, I strongly recommend using an advocate or private evaluator (see chapter 5) who is familiar with a severe discrepancy. Meet with them once you have your district's evaluation results as well as any information that you may have collected, and have the advocate or private evaluator attend your meeting with you.

The Team's Priority

In addition to 1 and 2 below, the remaining requirements are the same as those discussed in chapter 6 (see chapter 6 for more):

1. Your child is not achieving adequately in one or more of the following areas: oral expression, listening

comprehension, written expression, basic reading (phonemic awareness, phonics, vocabulary), reading fluency, reading comprehension, mathematics calculation, mathematics problem solving.

2. Your child exhibits a pattern of strengths and weaknesses in performance, achievement, or both, relative to age, state-approve, grade-level standards or intellectual development that is determined by a group to be relevant to the identification of a specific learning disability. (Here, strengths and weaknesses in achievement relative to intel-lectual development refer to a severe discrepancy.)

What the Team Will Pay Attention To

The team will pay particular attention to items 1 and 2. To determine if your child has a severe discrepancy, an evaluator will use a formula that compares your child's achievement results (1) to her IQ (2). They will be looking for evidence of unexpected underachievement discussed earlier.

Identify Your Child's Low Scores

When you request an evaluation for your child, ask for the district to send you its test results two days before the meeting (see sample letters 1 and 2 in appendix I). Wait until you receive those results before you meet with your advocate or private evaluator.

The first thing you'll want to do is review your child's standardized achievement results (1). Look for standard scores below 90, percentiles below 25, and scaled scores below 8 (see chapter 2 for more). They're the scores that will tell you your child is going to need extra support.

You won't be able to determine if your child meets your district's standard for a severe discrepancy (2) in advance of your meeting, however. If your child doesn't qualify for special education, you will still have identified your child's weaknesses and you can consider one of the options discussed at the end of chapter 2.

You and the advocate or private evaluator should review any other report you received from the school district or information you collected identifying low scores or comments referring to those scores (see chapter 6 for a list of tests and other relevant information in addition to 1 and 2, above).

When you find low scores on a standardized test, look for confirmation of those scores. For example, if reading comprehension, math problem solving, and written expression are low, look for confirmation of those scores, such as those found on private tests, state or district tests, an observation of your child, teacher comments, or work samples. The possibility of your child being eligible for special education will increase any time you have supporting evidence from multiple sources.

It's also important to note that some states or districts require RTI in addition to a severe discrepancy, where a severe discrepancy is used to determine eligibility. If you elected to use RTI, you'll want to review that information as well looking for a profile similar to Mason's, which was discussed in chapter 2.

Make a list your child's low scores and comments by professionals about those scores to take to your meeting. You'll also need to send a letter to the school district informing them a professional will attend the meeting with you. And I recommend developing a history of your child's testing and other relevant information once your child has an IEP (see chapter 6 for more detail).

Key Concepts

To understand how a team will determine your child's eligibility for special education using a severe discrepancy, you will need to know

- your state or district's requirements to determine eligibility using a severe discrepancy as well as IDEA's additional requirements;
- the advantages and disadvantages of a severe discrepancy;

- what information the team will consider to determine your child's eligibility;

- what information will support your child's eligibility for special education; and

- know what test sores and other relevant information you can take to your meeting that will support your child's eligibility.

Stress Check

We talked about a prescription for success in chapter 6. You can use the same approach here as well. Suppose your child does not qualify for special education but has test scores below 90, 25, and 8, indicating that she will need extra support. You and your advocate or private evaluator will want to consider the four options discussed at the end of chapter 2.

You'll want to consider an IEE if the team did not use a variety of assessments and strategies to determine your child's eligibility. You may also believe there were key assessments that were not used, or your child's evaluation was not comprehensive enough (see sample letter 3 in appendix I for more).

If you're satisfied that the assessments and strategies were thorough, you'll want to consider a remedial program in your district (after reviewing appendix IV), private tutoring, or a private summer program.

What's important is that your child's remedial or private program is intense and that you carry a genuine belief in her success.

You'll respond the same way if your child qualifies for special education. You'll advocate for intense services and monitor your child's progress carefully, and you'll couple this with your genuine belief in her success.

Your purpose is to place yourself in a position in which you'll be able to respond to whatever decision a team makes. This means you'll need to consider the scenarios above before your meeting takes place.

Advanced preparation, knowing that you're creating prescriptions for success for your child for any scenario will allow you to be relaxed about the outcome of your meeting.

Chapter 8
Attending a Meeting Where a Pattern of Strengths and Weaknesses is Used

A pattern of strengths and weaknesses is a classic approach used to determine LD. It allows a team great flexibility in determining eligibility for special education.

We have been discussing initial evaluation and re-evaluation meetings. So far, you've learned that a team may consider your child for special education in the LD category by using

- RTI
- another research-based intervention
- a severe discrepancy method

In this chapter, we'll look at the fourth method of determining eligibility. It's called a pattern of strengths and weaknesses (PSW) in school performance and academic achievement.

What is a Pattern of Strengths and Weaknesses?

A PSW is an approach that considers your child strengths and weaknesses in multiple areas of his performance and achievement in school and at home.

You can think of school performance as all of the subjective areas identified in chapter 4. They include:

- criterion-referenced testing by special education teachers (tests and quizzes)

- criterion-referenced testing by regular teachers (tests and quizzes)
- teacher's comments on a report card
- teacher's verbal comments
- report card grades
- an observation of your child in school
- your observation of your child at home
- your child's and family's history of LD

You can also think of academic achievement as all of the objective tests we identified in chapter 4. They include:

- standardized achievement tests
- progress monitoring (RTI)*
- work samples
- private testing
- district testing
- state testing
- reports on functional skills
- testing for a processing disorder

* Some states or districts will require RTI as part of its testing for a PSW.

Advantages and Disadvantages of a PSW

Advantages

One advantage of a PSW is that it's less likely that a small number of tests will have an important impact on eligibility. Instead, the team will weight objective and subjective information from many sources in making their decision.

Disadvantages

Similar to RTI and a severe discrepancy, a disadvantage is that there is no uniform standard used to determine a PSW. Your child may qualify for special education in one district or state and not in another.

Attending a Meeting Where a Pattern of Strengths and Weaknesses is Used

It will be important to collect information from as many sources as possible from the list of school performance and academic achievement tasks discussed above. I also strongly recommend using an advocate with the skills I discussed in chapter 5 for an initial evaluation or re-evaluation where your district will consider dropping your child. Meet with them once you have your district's evaluation results and have them attend the meeting with you.

The Team's Priority

In addition to 1 and 2 below, the remaining requirements are the same as those discussed in chapter 6 (see chapter 6 for more).

1. Your child is not achieving adequately in one or more of the following areas: oral expression, listening comprehension, written expression, basic reading (phonemic awareness, phonics, vocabulary), reading fluency, reading comprehension, mathematics calculation, mathematics problem solving.

2. There must be evidence that your child exhibits a PSW in performance, achievement, or both, relative to age or state-approved, grade-level standards or intellectual development that is determined by a group to be relevant to the identification of a specific learning disability.

What the Team Will Pay Attention To

To establish a PSW, the team will review school performance reports and results of academic achievement testing, such as those mentioned above. Strengths in academic achievement will frequently be determined by standardized tests with standard scores of 90 or above, and corresponding percentiles of 25 or scaled scores of 8. It's also usual to consider standard scores below 90, 25, and 8 respectively, as weaknesses (see chapter 2 for more). Teams will also use a variety of reports to establish strengths and weaknesses in school performance, such as report card grades, teacher comments, an observation of your child in school, or your child's and family's history.

Assuming strengths and weaknesses in school performance and/or academic achievement are found, your district may also evaluate your child using cognitive (mental) tests that are strongly related to achievement in reading, writing, and math. For example, if reading is a weakness, testing in the area of phonological awareness and rapid naming that focuses on beginning reading skills will be completed. If writing and spelling are weaknesses, tests of working memory and memory span, which are strongly related to written expression and spelling, will be completed.

Where weaknesses are found in cognitive and academic tests, and they are confirmed by other relevant information, it will support your child's eligibility in the LD category. These test results will most likely be found in a school psychologist's report. It's also usual to evaluate cognitive abilities globally (your child's general intelligence) to determine that low ability is not a cause of his weaknesses in achievement or performance.

Identify Your Child's Strengths and Weaknesses

Strengths

You and your advocate or private evaluator can prepare for your meeting by reviewing your district's tests and any additional information you have collected. Look for standard scores of 90 or above on standardized achievement tests (or percentiles of 25 or above or scaled scores of 8 or above). Look for those same standard scores on an intelligence test, if one was given.

Also look for strengths reported by regular or special education teachers or by a speech or occupational therapist if your child was tested for a functional skill. You'll want to document your child's strengths from your observations at home and in the community as well.

Think of factors such as your child's strengths in, social skills, or communication skills. Also think of strengths in cards or board games as well as your child's ability to catch on quickly if information is presented orally rather than in print.

Weaknesses

As discussed earlier, weaknesses on academic achievement (standardized) tests will be scores below 90, 25, and 8.

Weaknesses in school performance reports such as report cards, teacher comments or an observation of your child in the classroom will be identified by professionals in the school district reports that you receive before your meeting or those you may have collected.

Make sure to look for confirmation of weaknesses in academic achievement or school performance. For example, if reading fluency, spelling, math calculation, and written expression are weak on a standardized test, look for confirmation of those weaknesses from multiple sources, such as private testing, district testing, work samples, teacher comments, or report cards. The more sources you have confirming a weak score, the stronger your case for eligibility will be.

You'll want to make a list of your child's strengths and weaknesses to take to your meeting. And you will need to send a letter to the school district informing them a professional will attend your meeting with you. It will also be important to develop a history of your child's services if they qualify for special education (see chapter 6 for more detail).

Key Concepts

To understand how a team will determine your child's eligibility for special education using a PSW in school performance and academic achievement, you will need to know

- the IDEA requirements and your state or district's requirements to determine eligibility where a PSW in school performance and academic achievement is used;
- the different areas of school performance and academic achievement the team will investigate to identify a PSW;
- what information the team will pay attention to; and
- what information you can take to an IEP meeting that will support your child's eligibility for special education.

Stress Check

Preparing for a meeting is so important. The process of reviewing tests and other relevant information will give you a clear picture of your child's strengths and weaknesses. You will know where your child is going to need extra help in advance of your meeting. You can also review with your advocate how you will respond if he doesn't qualify for special education.

Regardless of the outcome of your meeting, you'll want to make sure your child has intense services coupled with your belief in his success. You will see a positive change as your child starts to make progress. And he will eventually take ownership of his progress and his success. There is no greater reward than to see that happen. You will know clearly that your child is capable of being productive and successful in life.

Chapter 9
Requesting an Increase in Services

You can be successful requesting an increase in services if you have evidence of regression from multiple sources supported by other relevant information.

You've now been through the process of applying your foundation skills to initial evaluations and re-evaluations. Those same skills can be used to help you negotiate increased services for your child or for a change of placement.

In this chapter, we'll look at requesting an increase in services. It's such an important topic not only because it's vital to your child's progress but it also has such a high potential to cause stress.

Unfortunately, parents have heard so many negative comments about requesting increased services that they assume that's what will happen with their child. They forget that their child has a unique set of skills that must be looked at individually by a team. Parents also don't take into consideration their ability to influence the outcome of a meeting. Let's take a closer look at how you can do that.

Using Support

The first time you request an increase in services I recommend using an advocate with the skills I discussed in chapter 5 (See item 3 in table 5.1). You should meet with them before your IEP meeting and have them attend your meeting with you.

You can also use a private evaluator as your advocate if you have had your child tested privately. Make sure to meet with them before your meeting and have them attend the meeting with you as well.

You learned in chapters 6, 7, and 8 that it was important to collect test results and other relevant information once your child has an IEP to develop a history of her services. Do you have standardized achievement test results from two or more years of testing from special education?

You may recall that you can compare the standard scores to document regression (a decrease in scores from one year to the next). You'll be looking for evidence of regression from standardized tests and other relevant information (see chapter 2 for more on closing the gap in skills).

Collect Objective Information Each Year

One of the things you'll need to do as you collect information is request standardized achievement testing by special education each year. That will allow you to keep track of your child's progress using objective test data.

That may sound like a lot testing for a special education teacher, but you don't need to have all the subtests on a test completed every year. You can request testing in those areas in which your child has goals and objectives in her IEP. For example, if your child has goals and objectives in spelling, reading fluency, math calculation, and math problem solving, ask for testing in those areas.

For a re-evaluation, ask for a complete test using the same test that was given at your child's initial evaluation. Why? You'll ask for a complete test to confirm your child's progress (or lack of progress) and to make sure she hasn't lost skills in other areas over a three-year period.

Use Evidence from Multiple Sources

The list below shows possible tests and other relevant information you can gather about your child that will support your request for increased services.

- standardized achievement testing by special education
- private standardized achievement testing

- district standardized achievement testing *
- state test
- teacher's comments at an IEP meeting

* District testing refers to testing of regular education students. It's usually given at a particular grade level and sometimes to multiple grade levels. You receive the results of those tests.

Consider an Individually Administered Test First

The tests that will provide the strongest support for your request to increase services are special education standardized achievement testing and/or private testing. Why? They're strong because they are individually administered tests and provide standard scores needed to document regression.

You may be in the position of comparing standardized testing by special education to a private test. Look first for evidence that both tests show regression in the same skills. For example, there may be evidence from special education testing that your child has regressed in spelling, written expression, and reading fluency. Look for evidence of regression in those same skills in your child's private standardized achievement testing.

It's also possible for a private test to identify weak skills not found in special education testing. When that happens, the team will need to decide how to resolve the difference in scores.

Consider a District or State Test Second

District or state tests are also useful for supporting weaknesses found in special education or private standardized testing. Using our example above, you can look for evidence of regression in spelling, written expression, and fluency on a district or state test as well. The more evidence you have confirming regression in specific skills from multiple objective tests, the more strength you will put behind your request.

Look for Regression from Subjective Sources

A teacher may also comment on your child's difficulty mastering one or more of the skills identified in a special education standardized test, a private test, or a district or state test. That confirmation will support your request for increased services as well. You can look for confirmation of weak skills from other sources such as work samples, RTI or an observation of your child in school as well.

The Team's Decision

It will be difficult for a team to argue against an increase in services if you and the advocate or private evaluator present standardized test results showing declining scores from multiple sources supported by other relevant information.

If the team refuses your request, you can ask for mediation (see chapter 3 for more). You'll be in a strong position to reach a positive outcome because of the information you will have collected.

When to Request Increased Services

You can request increased services whenever you have evidence of regression. This means that you can request an increase in services one year after your child's initial evaluation as long as you have the evidence we discuss above to support it.

When to Consider Other Options

Consider other options when your advocate feels that more information is needed to support your request for increased services. One option is for the advocate to observe your child in an inclusion (services given in a regular classroom) or pullout program (services given outside of a regular classroom). They will know what information will support your request.

The advocate may also recommend a private evaluation in place of an observation or in addition to it. Even though that may delay your request, follow their advice so you have the best possible chance of success.

Key Concepts

To be successful requesting an increase in services, you will need to know

- what skills and training you will need from an advocate to support your request;
- what information to collect annually that will support your request;
- when to request an increase in services; and
- when an observation or private evaluation will support for your request.

Stress Check

Parents frequently believe that their request for increased services will be refused resulting in stress.

It's important to wait until you have evidence of regression before you request an increase in services. You should not make a request if you're relying on special education's most recent criterion-referenced testing, a district test, or a state test.

You may recall that most criterion-referenced tests are not objective (they're not reliable or valid). Also, district and state tests are not considered as reliable as an individually administered test because they are given in a group setting.

If you don't have two or more years of individually administered standardized achievement results, I recommend having your child tested privately before you make your request. You always want to walk into a meeting in the strongest possible position to have your requests approved.

This means making sure you have the right test information to support your request. You'll also know that you have convincing evidence to go to mediation if the team refuses your request. You can walk into any meeting feeling optimistic about the outcome when you have taken the steps discussed in this chapter.

Chapter 10
Requesting a Placement in LD Self-Contained Program

Proper placement is about making sure the services offered will meet your child's unique needs. Placement should not be based on a teacher's reputation or the recommendation of a parent.

You may be aware that public school self-contained LD programs are increasing as an alternative to LD day placements. For those who are not familiar with self- contained or day programs, a self-contained LD program is located in a public school and provides direct instruction in basic skills (reading, writing, and math) as well as support for those skills in other core subjects such as science and social studies.

An LD day placement is located in a separate setting, and provides direct instruction in all core subjects (reading, writing, math, science, and social studies).

The good news for parents is that the public school self-contained programs are attempting to provide services similar to a day placement. This doesn't mean that your district's self-contained program is able to do that, however.

It will require a careful investigation to know if a self-contained program will meet your child's needs. If you're reading this chapter, you may be thinking about a self-contained LD program for your child. To make your decision, you'll need to take three important steps.

Your first step will be to consider your child's readiness for a LD self-contained program. Then you'll have to make sure you have the right testing and other relevant information to support a placement.

Your third step will be to carefully evaluate your district's program. Let's look at each step.

Step 1: Consider Your Child's Readiness

Self-contained LD programs are found at all levels in a district. Most, however, are at the middle- school level. Middle-school is certainly not the best time to consider a referral but it may become necessary for the student with LD who has moderate to severe needs.

I say that because the demands of the curriculum may reach a point where they will outpace your child's ability to keep up. That typically happens in fifth or sixth grade. How will you know if it's time to consider a referral? You'll know if your child is experiencing a combination of the following behaviors:

- Your child is experiencing considerable difficulty keeping up with daily homework, reading assignments, reports, or projects.
- There are multiple signs of stress at home, such as angry outbursts, frequent crying, withdrawal, unhappiness, or high levels of anxiety about not being able to meet timelines. Your child may also not want to go to school.
- There are reports that your child is reacting in school by refusing to go to a special education group inside or outside of the classroom, not working on homework in school in his area(s) of weakness, not sharing his work with others or is sensitive about working in small groups.

The above are signs that your child can't keep up in spite of his wish to do so. And he is doing everything possible protect himself from being embarrassed in front of his peers. If you're seeing the above behaviors, it's time to take the second step by looking at what evidence you have to support a referral to your district's self-contained program.

Step 2: Look for Evidence of Regression

You learned in chapter 9 that to support a request for a referral, you'll need to have two or more years of evidence that your child is regressing. Your ideal circumstance will be if your child is presently receiving intense services and you also have evidence of regression.

Intense services means services given four or five days per week in a group of four or less. It will include a minimum of 45 to 60 minutes a day for reading or 75 to 90 minutes for reading and writing. Mathematics will be an additional 45 to 60 minutes and reading fluency will be an additional 15 to 20 minutes per day if your child has needs in those areas.

I recommend intense services because if your child is already receiving intense services and you have evidence he's not making adequate progress (evidence of regression), you'll increase your chances significantly that the IEP team will approve your child's placement.

If your child is not receiving intense services, it's highly likely that the team will recommend increasing his services in place of approving a placement. I strongly recommend using an advocate for that meeting (see item 4 in table 5.1). A question you can ask is, will the proposed increase be enough to meet your child's unique needs. If you and the advocate agree that it will be enough (using the definition of intense services above as a guide), you will monitor your child's progress and have him tested at the end of the year making sure the district uses an individually administered standardized test. Ask the district to use the same standardized test that was previous given to your child so you will be comparing apples to apples.

If you have evidence of regression from that testing, ask for a placement in your district's self-contained program. It will very likely be approved. On the other hand, you and the advocate will want to consider mediation if the team does not recommend intense service that will meet your child's needs using the definition above as a guide (see chapter 3 for more on mediation).

Step 3: Investigate your District's Program

The third step you'll need to take will be to thoroughly investigate your district's self-contained LD program. It will not be enough for you to talk with the LD program staff or to read about the program. I strongly recommend using one of the advocates referred to in chapter 5 to observe the program as well.

You'll need to make a written request to observe a self-contained LD program to the director of special education in your district. You can use sample letter 5 in appendix I as a guide to write your letter.

Schedule an Observation

You can call your state department of special education to find out what your rights are regarding an observation. Each state has guidelines. I recommend an observation because there are many aspects of the self-contained program you'll miss if you limit your search to a discussion or a paper review.

For example, you won't know where the LD program is located or what the physical environment is like. You will also not know what the classroom atmosphere is like. Classroom atmosphere refers to things such as how the physical space is arranged to promote learning, the level of comfort students have with each other and the teacher, the impact some students may have on learning for others, and the general tone of the classroom that is set by the teacher.

You may also recall from chapter 5 that your advocate will have experience teaching basic skills, and be skilled in research-based instruction (or they will have a good understanding of basic skills and research-based instruction). They will also be skilled at interpreting achievement test results in addition to their skill at observing programs.

An advocate with the above skills will know if the teacher of the self-contained program is using appropriate teaching and monitoring methods to meet students' unique needs. They will also know if the classroom atmosphere is appropriate and the tone of the classroom set by the teacher is relaxed yet focused on learning.

The Elements of a Well-Designed Program

Table 10.1 is a list of the elements of a well-designed LD self-contained program. It's accompanied by a separate form (table 10.2) that can be used to record comments. You can share it with the advocate.

Table 10.1 Checklist to observe a district LD self-contained program or an LD day school		
Instructions: Check the appropriate box for each question. Use the attached page to record comments. Check One: This form is being used to observe an _____LD Self-Contained Program _____an LD Day School Name of Observer _____ Date _____		
Does the LD self-contained program (or day school) have the following elements?	YES	NO
1 A strong focus on basic skill improvement accompanied by an emphasis on effective student progress in the classroom curriculum.		
2 Research-based instruction is used and it is used with fidelity (the way it's intended).		
3 Instruction is explicit and systematic. Explicit means that skills are clearly explained and modeled. Systematic means skills are taught in a planned appropriate sequence with frequent opportunity to practice.		
4 Instruction is organized so students can build on past teaching with enough practice so they can internalize the skills they are learning.		
5 Basic skill work is given intensively daily. Intensively means a minimum of 45 to 60 minutes for reading, 75 to 90 minutes for reading and writing, 45 to 60 minutes for mathematics, and 15 to 20 minutes for fluency.		
6 Monitoring student progress is frequent— at least every two weeks.		
7 Adjustments are made in the method of instruction when test results (data) confirm that progress is not being made. That will include adjustments such as increasing the amount of time for instruction and/or decreasing the size of a group.		
8 All professional staff are trained to use the same research-based instructional methods as well as progress monitoring assessments.		
9 Group size for basic skill instruction is held to a maximum of four students.		
10 Groups are organized based on similar skill needs.		
11 Basic skills are reinforced across the curriculum including science and social studies.		
12 The classroom atmosphere is relaxed yet focused on learning.		
13 There is an option for a student to receive individual counseling.		
14 There is a social skills group to improve student awareness of appropriate social skills. It includes discussing LD issues that occur within the program and that students encounter in other settings.		

	Table 10.2 Chart to record comments when observing an LD self-contained program or an LD day school
1	
2	
3	
4	
5	
6	
7	
8	
9	
10	
11	
12	
13	
14	

These are the elements the advocate will look for when they observe your district's self-contained program. If the elements are not present or not used the way they're intended, the advocate may recommend a day placement. We'll discuss day placements in chapter 11. Table 10.1 can also be used to observe an LD day school (more on that later).

Prepare Your Child

It's important to let your child know that you're looking at an LD self-contained program. He will be receptive if he's experiencing the kind of stress I discussed in step one. As you learn about the program from your advocate's observations, you can share it with your child. You can also request permission for your child to spend a day in the program once a placement has been approved. Most students come away from that experience with positive feelings. They understand it's an environment where they can get the help they need.

When to Consider Alternatives

The profile of your child's readiness that I discuss in step one makes it easy to decide to move forward and investigate your district's self-contained program. However, what if your child's profile is a mix of the following positive behaviors accompanied by significant skill weaknesses and he resists placement in a self-contained program?

- Your child has excellent social skills.
- You child has definite strengths in academic areas such as math and science.
- Your child is a good athlete.
- Your child has a talent in music, art, drama, or technology.

When your child has skills and/or talent in a number of the above areas and they resist placement, you can consider other alternatives. For example, if you have evidence of regression, you can request an increase in services in his current program in place of requesting a self-contained program. You can also consider private tutoring to work on skills and to support your child's daily assignments. If your child is still not making adequate progress (you have evidence of regression) by the end of the year, you can reconsider a self-contained program.

Key Concepts

To understand what you need to consider when you look into in an LD self-contained program, you will need to know

- that your child is ready for a change of placement;
- what testing and other relevant information you will need for your child to be accepted into a self-contained program; and
- if the self-contained program will meet your child's unique needs.

Stress Test

Considering a self-contained program requires careful planning because it will remove your child from the mainstream. When you use a structured approach such as the three steps and the support of an advocate described in this chapter, it will allow you to make an informed decision.

Proper preparation is a key to having your request approved. When you've prepared properly and you have the support of an advocate, you will feel relaxed and confident as you move through the steps.

Involving your child will allow him to feel he's an important part of the process as well. It will also be a beautiful demonstration to your child of how to go about making an informed decision, where the stakes are high and your child's self-esteem is an important dimension.

Chapter 11
Requesting a Placement in an LD Day School

There are two significant signs of the need for a day placement—your child's failure to make progress in the presence of intense services and their emotional distress.

It's more difficult to place your child in an LD day school because public schools are creating their own LD self-contained programs. The chances are good that your district has at least one LD self-contained program.

That makes it a challenge for parents who want to place their child in a day school. It doesn't place it out of reach, however. It simply means you'll have to be aware of your child's progress and plan carefully before you make a request for a placement. Let's look at how you will do that.

A Profile of a Child with Severe LD

Your child can actually be identified in the early grades if she has the profile of a child who may attend a day school (a profile of a child with severe needs). Although there will be signs of difficulty in kindergarten, you may not be fully aware of the extent of your child's LD until the middle of first grade.

Reports from your child's first grade teacher will show that your child is not making progress learning to read. Because of that, her beginning writing and spelling will also be well behind her peers. Your child's difficulty learning to read and write will continue into second and third grade. It is very likely your child's teacher in these grades will encourage you to refer your child for a special education evaluation if you haven't done so already.

Your child will still be working on beginning reading and writing skills by the end of third grade if she has not received help. She will have made some progress if she has been accepted into special education but her skills will very likely still be at first-grade level.

As your child moves into fourth, fifth, and sixth grade, her program will need to be adjusted each year to accommodate her weak reading and writing and possibly math skills. That means your child may have to take tests orally and have grade-level material read to her or tape recorded in order for her to participate in the classroom curriculum.

If there's an LD self-contained program at the elementary level, there's a good chance your child will be referred to it. By third grade your child will already be aware that her skills are different from those of her peers. This means the chances are great that she will have formed a belief about her learning discussed in chapter 1 and that belief may impact her self-esteem.

If she continues in a pullout or inclusion program in fourth, fifth, or sixth grade, the skill differences between her and her peers will be magnified further each year. You, of course, will be very aware of your child's weaknesses because of the level of stress she will experience completing work at home. You may even find you have become a second teacher, just so your child can complete homework assignments.

Refer Your Child Early

You won't have to worry about referring your child early (first or second grade) or worry that she may not qualify for special education because her skill weaknesses will be so pronounced. Refer your child by February of first grade if the school district has not (at the time of her second report card).

As I discussed in chapter 4, you'll need to monitor your child's progress and collect the objective and subjective information from the time special education services begin.

This is important, because special education pullout or inclusion programs may not offer the intense services initially that we described in chapter 10. And your child will not make adequate progress unless her services are intense over an extended period of time.

Monitor Services Frequently

You are likely to find yourself in the position of asking for an increase in services annually. To do that, you'll need to have the evidence of regression discussed in chapter 9. Even when your child's services are at an intense level, you'll need to continue to monitor her progress and collect evidence.

You will do this because there is no guarantee that the intense services offered will be enough. So, continue to ask for standardized achievement testing each year and collect all of the other information I discussed in chapter 4.

Ideally, your child should be accepted into special education in first or second grade and should be receiving intense services by third grade at the latest. The end of third grade is the ideal time to request a day placement.

Self-Contained vs. Day Placements

If you have evidence that your child is still not making adequate progress (evidence of regression) once she's receiving intense services, you'll need to decide if your next step will be to request an LD self-contained program in your district or an LD day placement.

Your district will want you to refer your child to a self-contained program first if there is one that provides services at your child's grade level. You, on the other hand, may want to refer your child immediately to a day placement.

To refer your child immediately, I strongly recommend using an advocate or attorney, described in chapter 5. They may recommend hiring an expert to observe the LD self-contained program and the day school.

Why both? You'll need to compare programs to build a case for a placement in a day program. The elements of a well-designed LD self-contained program, which I discussed in chapter 10 are also true for a day placement. The advocate's review of both programs will provide important evidence that may support a day placement.

Look for Evidence of Regression

You'll need to gather evidence of regression from as many of the objective and subjective sources of information described in chapter 4 as you can. Your advocate or attorney will welcome that evidence.

They may, however, also recommend a private evaluation if they believe there's not enough current objective information. It's important to follow their advice. They will know what evidence will best support a day placement.

When a Placement Is Refused

Your district may not agree with a placement in a day school. Then you'll need to decide with your advocate or attorney whether to accept the district's recommendation or request a due process hearing. Consider a due process hearing when you have the following evidence and the recommendation of your advocate or attorney:

- You have strong evidence of regression from both objective and subjective sources.
- You have thoroughly investigated the district's self-contained program and day school and you have strong evidence that the day placement is the only option that meets your child's unique needs (more below).
- Your child is highly stressed about not being able to keep up with daily work and about going to school. Making progress in the regular education curriculum from fifth grade forward will very likely require an excessive number of accommodations.

Those accommodations, such as oral tests or tape recorded textbooks, will make her look different at a time when she will want to look and act the same as her peers.

Building Your Case for a Day Placement

I mentioned above that you must have strong evidence that the district's self-contained program will not meet your child's needs. What I mean is that you'll need to make a case that many of the elements of the district's LD self-contained program described in chapter 10 are not present or if they are present, they're not used the way they're intended.

This means the district's program does not

- use research-based instruction with fidelity,
- teach skills explicitly or systematically,
- provide frequent practice of skills so they are internalized,
- monitor progress frequently,
- keep group size to a maximum of four students, and
- reinforce basic skills across the curriculum.

When a District's Program is Appropriate

Your advocate may find that the district's LD self-contained program contains all of the elements of a well-designed program. If that's the case, it will be a wise choice to place your child in it. Your child will be receiving the same program she would have received in a day placement.

Your child will require a period of adjustment. However, once she realizes that she can get the help she needs and make progress, she will quickly adapt to her new environment.

Your first choice will always be for your child to be educated in her home school. It's only when a public school isn't able to provide a program to meet your child's unique needs that you will want to look at other options.

Key Concepts

To understand what you will need to do to place your child in a LD day school you will need to

- be alert to the severity of your child's needs in the early grades;
- monitor your child's progress carefully;
- gather evidence to build a case for a placement in a day school;
- use expert support to help you make decisions as you move toward a placement;
- know what your options are if a placement is refused; and
- know how to determine if your district's placement is appropriate.

Stress Check

Deciding on a day placement requires careful planning and carries the potential for stress. It's important to keep all options open as you move toward a day placement. If your district has used its resources to build an excellent program, it will be the best placement for your child.

Carrying a fixed idea about what will happen will only heighten your stress and then you'll be disappointed if it doesn't turn out the way you imagined. Instead of carrying a belief that a day placement is the only option for your child, carry the belief that you will find a placement that meets your child's unique needs. Then you'll be satisfied with the outcome regardless of what happens.

Chapter 12
Section 504 Referrals

You will need to prepare for a 504 meeting as well as you would for an IEP meeting. The stakes are as great for your child.

Meeting 504 Requirements

There are some children who won't need the specialized instruction offered by special education but will require other services to help them function in school. They're children with physical or mental disabilities who may be eligible for services provided through a separate law called Section 504 of the Rehabilitation Acts of 1973 (referred to as Section 504). Section 504 is a civil rights law that's enforced by the Office of Civil Rights, an agency in the US Department of Education.

To be eligible under Section 504, your child must have a physical or mental impairment that substantially limits one or more major life activities. Major life activities include areas such as caring for oneself, walking, seeing, hearing, speaking, breathing, learning, concentrating, thinking, and communicating. The list below is an example of the kinds of impairments that may qualify for Section 504 services. The list is not exhaustive.

- abuse of drugs or alcohol
- AIDS
- students with allergies or asthma who miss school frequently
- an emotional disability
- an environmental illness
- an illness or injury that will require hospitalization or homebound services

- ADHD
- bipolar disorder
- cancer
- cerebral palsy
- chronic fatigue syndrome
- communicable diseases (e.g., hepatitis)
- cystic fibrosis
- diabetes
- dwarfism
- encopresis/enuresis
- epilepsy
- hearing impairment
- heart disease
- leukemia
- migraine headaches
- muscular dystrophy
- orthopedic conditions
- special health care needs
- speech impairment
- Tourette's syndrome
- traumatic brain injury
- tuberculosis
- vision impairment
- weight issues, such as obesity, anorexia, bulimia

Consider Special Education Services First

You should always consider whether to refer your child for special education before you make a referral for Section 504 services. If your child has a physical or mental impairment and he's having difficulty with a basic skill (reading, writing, spelling, or math), you'll want to refer him for special education first. If you're unsure, refer him for special education. It's better to have a team rule out special education than to assume your child won't qualify. If your child doesn't qualify for special education, the team may recommend a Section 504 referral.

There's a checklist at the end of this chapter (table 12.2) that will cover all of the key points I discuss. Use it to help prepare for a 504 meetings about your child. So focus on this chapter's content; all of the key information will be available to you when you need it.

Examples of 504 Eligibility Decisions

The fact that your child has a physical or mental impairment won't be enough for him to qualify for Section 504 services. His impairment must substantially limit a major life activity. Let's look at some examples of how he might qualify for Section 504 services:

Your child is diagnosed with cerebral palsy and uses a battery powered wheelchair. You believe he'll need an adult with him full time during the day at school. The team will need to consider whether an adult is needed full or part time. For example, will he need an adult with him while he's attending a class?

The team's primary concern will be your child's safety as well as his access to the building and all normal school functions. Those will include functions such as getting to and from classes, on and off a bus, in and out of the building and using bathrooms, lockers, drinking fountains, and the cafeteria. It will also include participating in activities such as art, music, PE, and clubs that are available to all students.

Looking at the definition of Section 504, the team will consider if your child's physical impairment (cerebral palsy) substantially limits a major life activity (walking) and as a result he is unable to take part in normal school activities and requires an adult to be present full time. This example will apply to other impairments on list above that may limit a child's mobility, such as orthopedic conditions and muscular dystrophy.

Another example: your child is diagnosed with ADD and there's a recommendation from private testing for a behavior management program to help him pay attention during class. His grades have dropped. You referred him for a special education evaluation but he didn't qualify.

Looking at the definition of Section 504, the team will consider if your child's mental impairment (ADD) substantially limits a major life activity (learning) and has caused his grades to drop. If you review the list above, you'll see a large number of impairments that have the potential to affect learning. Some may affect learning as a result of a child missing a large number of days in a school year. Impairments such as chronic fatigue syndrome or asthma fit this category.

Other impairments may affect a child's ability to concentrate (and as a result his ability to learn). They're impairments such as bipolar disorder or Tourette's syndrome. In each case the team will look at whether your child's physical or mental impairment substantially limits a major life activity.

Home or Hospital Tutoring

Another physical impairment on the list is for students who have had an accident, surgery, or an illness and will need to be in a hospital or at home. Those students may be eligible for tutoring services to help them keep up to date with schoolwork.

To qualify for 504 services a student must actually be at home or in a hospital for more than 6 months or he must be expected to be away that long. If his stay at home or in a hospital is expected to be less than 6 months, he may still be eligible for home tutoring services.

Those services are treated separately from 504 and are called home and hospital services. You can read more about home and hospital services in appendix III.

Student Accommodation Plan

Table12.1 is an example of a Section 504 student accommodation plan. An accommodation plan is a document completed by a team to determine if a student qualifies for 504 services and lists the services he will receive.

Although most school districts have a document, it's important to note that Section 504 does not require a written plan. The description that follows, therefore, is what typically happens, not what is required by Section 504.

Table 12.1 SECTION 504 STUDENT ACCOMMODATION PLAN

Student: _____ DOB: _____
School: _____ Date: _____
Team Chairperson: _____
Justification for Services

1. Does the student have a physical or mental impairment which substantially limits one or more major life activities?

   ___ YES ___ NO

   Check all major life activities that apply.

   _ caring for oneself _ hearing _ thinking
   _ performing manual tasks _ speaking _ communicating
   _ walking _ working
   _ seeing _ learning _ other _____
   _ breathing _ concentrating

2. Document the basis for determining the disability.

   _____
   _____
   _____
   _____
   _____

3. Describe the accommodations that will be provided.
   Accommodation
   _____
   Accommodation
   _____
   Accommodation
   _____
   Accommodation
   _____

I give permission for my child to receive the above mentioned services.
   _____Parent   Date _____
Describe why the child does not qualify for Section 504 services if question 1 is answered No.

   _____
   _____
   _____

It's typical for a team to focus on the definition of a child with a disability under Section 504 (questions 1 and 2) and then address the services that will be provided (question 3).

The team will also document why your child did not qualify for Section 504 services if the answer to question 1 is no. Notice that the plan is called a student accommodation plan. What are accommodations? They're adjustments that are made to take into account your child's physical or mental impairment without reducing learning expectations.

It means he'll learn the same academic content as his peers, but may need extra time to take tests because of a physical impairment, or he may need to take a test in a quiet environment due to a mental impairment. Providing extra time or a quiet environment are accommodations.

The purpose of accommodations is to allow your child to compete on an equal level with his peers. Most Section 504 plans will have content similar to the accommodation plan in table 12.1. The one your district uses may look different, however, as there's no requirement for states to create a uniform Section 504 document.

The following websites will give you a better idea of the types of accommodations used for different physical or mental impairments.

- South Lane School District–Section 504 Sample Accommodations and Modifications
- Guidelines for Educators and Administrators for Implementing Section 504 of the Rehabilitation Act of 1973-Subpart D

Additional 504 Services

Your child may also receive modifications, related services, supplementary aids and services, or special education and related services under a 504 plan. Let's look at each.

Modifications

Modifications change or reduce learning expectations. Since modifications change learning expectations, your child will learn less of the content than his peers. Teams will decide on a case-by-case basis whether a modification is acceptable for your child to receive a passing grade in elementary or middle school or to receive credit in high school.

It may mean that he'll require an extra year to graduate if he's attending high school. Modifications are typically considered for conditions such as a serious illness, injury, or major surgery, where the student is expected to be absent from school for long periods of time.

Related Services

Related services are services such as occupational therapy, physical therapy, speech therapy, counseling, and medical diagnostic services. They're usually given outside the classroom and may need to be coordinated with out-of-school medical or psychological services.

Related services should be planned so that they have a minimum impact on core subjects (English, math, science, and social studies/history).

Supplementary Aids and Services

Supplementary aids and services are services such as interpreters for the deaf, taped books or readers for the blind, transportation, voice dictate programs or adapted keyboards for students who are unable to write or have difficulty writing.

They may also include nursing services or the use of trained aides for students with medical needs. For students with substantial needs, much time is spent initially working on logistics (coordinating all of the services) to make sure they have their needs met and at the same time can feel they are part of a normal school day.

Special Education and Related Services

You also read earlier that Section 504 may include special education and related services. What do I mean? Some districts will write a special education plan if your child needs basic skills instruction.

They will also write a 504 plan for a related service, such as speech or occupational therapy. Although this is done, it's not necessary to write two plans if your child qualifies for special education. All of his services can be part of an IEP.

If your child qualifies for special education, you should request that all of his services become part of his IEP. You have more rights under special education than Section 504.

The primary differences between the federal special education law referred to as the IDEA and Section 504 are as follows:

IDEA	Section 504
A referral occurs when a disability adversely affects educational performance	A referral occurs when a physical or mental impairment substantially limits one or more major life activities
A team conducts a comprehensive evaluation of all areas of suspected disability.	A team conducts a review of records and may evaluate a student in an area of suspected need.
A parent must be invited to an initial evaluation, annual review, or a re-evaluation every three years.	A district must notify a parent if they intend to identify, evaluate, or place a child. There is no requirement for a parent to attend a meeting
If accepted into services, a team will write an IEP.	If accepted into services, a team will typically write (but is not required to write) an accommodation plan.
Uses specially designed instruction for a student to make adequate progress in IEP goals and the curriculum.	Uses accommodations so a student will have access to programs and activities offered to all students. There is no requirement for progress to be made

Figure 12.1. Comparison of the IDEA and Section 504

Your Rights under Section 504

If you have a disagreement over your child's services, you'll have a right to file a complaint with the 504 coordinator for your district. You'll also be able to request a due process hearing (see chapter 3 for more) or file a complaint with the Office for Civil Rights. The district must also notify you if they intend to identify, evaluate, or place your child.

It's also important to note that there's no requirement for parents to attend 504 meetings. Each school district makes a decision regarding parent attendance. You'll know whether parents are included because your district must prepare a 504 procedures manual that will be available through the superintendent's office (also called a board of education office).

There should be a statement about parent attendance in that manual. Note: Most districts welcome parent attendance and participation in 504 meetings.

When you refer your child for a 504 evaluation, you'll receive a copy of your rights. If you would like to know them in advance, you'll find your rights in your district's 504 procedures manual.

An important benefit of Section 504 services is that its protections don't stop at age 22, as those for special education do. They extend for the life of your disabled child and protect him from discrimination in areas such as employment, access to buildings, transportation, and higher education.

Submitting Documentation

You'll need a letter from your doctor stating your child's diagnosis, whether or not you're able to participate in a 504 meeting. You can also submit evidence in writing with the help of someone knowledgeable. If you're able to participate, you or an advocate can present evidence at your meeting.

If your child will need home or hospital tutoring (discussed earlier) and will be out of school for more than six months or is expected to be out for that long, the doctor's letter must state that as well. The letter should also request home or hospital tutoring. The district 504 coordinator's office may have a letter describing what a doctor must submit. Give that letter to your doctor's office.

The letter from your doctor or specialist needs to be sent to the 504 coordinator in your district. Note: Make sure you request the letter from your doctor well in advance of your meeting. Doctors' offices are usually slow when submitting this kind of information.

You may have the same difficulty if your child is transitioning from a hospital to home and will still need tutoring for an extended time. When that happens, your doctor may need to send an additional letter. You can find that out from the 504 coordinator.

Make sure to request the letter well in advance of your child leaving the hospital. Also alert the 504 coordinator of a discharge date from the hospital and the need to have home tutoring in place as soon after that date as possible.

The District's Review

The school district will complete a review of your child's records and may conduct its own evaluation. If the school district evaluates your child, it must be on an individual basis. The team will look for recommendations from staff members who have regular contact with your child.

As you learned earlier, a medical diagnosis will not be enough for him to qualify for Section 504 services. His physical or mental impairment must substantially limit a major life activity.

Attending with an Advocate

I recommend taking an advocate to your first 504 meeting. Try to find someone who has had experience with Section 504. You can use sample letter 4 in appendix I to notify the school district that a professional will attend the meeting with you. Make sure your letter arrives at least two days before your meeting.

You also need to spend time with the advocate developing a list of the accommodations you believe your child will need. Take that list to your meeting, and be prepared to request accommodations where it seems appropriate.

Locating Appropriate Personnel

You can call the superintendent's office (it may be called a board of education) to find out who is responsible for Section 504 services. That office will have a form that you can use to refer your child. If he qualifies for 504 services, the team will write an accommodation plan similar to the one in table 12.1 listing the services he'll receive.

504 services are usually a regular education responsibility. A guidance counselor or assistant principal, therefore, may be your contact person for meetings or to discuss other concerns. They'll very likely be the chairperson of meetings as well.

You can use the checklist in table 12.2 to prepare for a 504 meeting about your child.

Table 12.2 Section 504 Checklist				
Instructions: Place a check in the appropriate box for each question. Use the comments section for reminders of important dates or follow-up activities. Use NA for any question that is not applicable				
504 Meeting	Yes	No	NA	Comments
Do you have the name and phone number of the person in charge of 504 referrals for your district?				
Have you received a form from that office to request a 504 evaluation?				
Have you followed up if you did not receive a form within a few days?				
Has your doctor sent a letter to the 504 coordinator with a diagnosis of your child's physical or mental impairment?				
If your child will require home and hospital tutoring, is there also a statement in the letter that he will be out of school for more than six months?				
Have you allowed plenty of time for your doctor to send a letter to your district's 504 coordinator?				
Have you followed up if the doctor has not sent a letter?				
Will you take an advocate to the meeting with you?				
If so, have you sent a letter to the 504 coordinator that will arrive at least two days in advance of the meeting, stating a professional will attend the meeting with you?				
Have you consulted with the advocate about the accommodations you believe your child will need?				
If so, have you created a list of the accommodations to take to the meeting?				
Have you discussed who will present those accommodations?				

Key Concepts

To refer your child for Section 504 you should

- first consider a referral for special education;
- inform yourself about Section 504 through your district's 504 procedures manual;
- have a letter sent to the district from your doctor stating your child's diagnosis;

- follow your district's instructions regarding what must be in a letter from your doctor if your child will need home or hospital tutoring;
- use an advocate for your first 504 meeting; and
- go to the meeting with a list of accommodations you believe your child will need.

Stress Check

The process for requesting and receiving 504 services is less complicated than it is for special education. However, that doesn't mean it will be less stressful for some parents. Your best approach to reduce stress will be to find proper support and then focus your attention developing appropriate accommodations for your child.

In chapter 1 you learned that your child's belief in success and intensive services go together. In the same way, when your child has a physical or mental impairment, his belief in success and appropriate accommodations go together. If a belief in success is missing or accommodations are not appropriate or not used, they can impact your child's self-esteem and his progress.

When your child believes he's successful, he'll actively advocate for himself in the classroom or in other activities such as art, music, gym, sports, clubs, or field trips. Although he'll be aware of his limitations, he'll adapt them to the situation to make the best use of his physical or mental abilities. To put it another way, he'll look for opportunities to be successful at all times.

His success will reinforce his view of himself as successful, which, in turn, will lead to more success. So, in addition to carrying a genuine belief in your child's success, you'll need to request a review of his accommodations annually. That's important, because some accommodations may no longer be relevant and will need to be dropped or modified.

Afterword

Being the Best That You Can Be

There's a lot of knowledge to absorb in *Becoming Your Child's Best Advocate*. However, you don't need to learn it all in one reading. Remember that this book was designed to take you through the special education process.

This means that there will be sections of the book that will be relevant now and other sections that will be relevant after your child has an IEP. You can, therefore, use the book as a useful reference as you encounter each new phase of your child's services.

Also remember that because much of what is introduced are strategies you can use to make the process easier and to ensure success, they will be as relevant and useful five years from now as they are today.

Becoming Your Child's Best Advocate focuses strongly on building your knowledge. That's so important because it will allow you to be on the same level as other team members. You'll no longer feel that you're an outsider to the team process. Instead, you'll be able to actively participate in IEP team meetings and make requests based on sound evidence.

When you gather strong evidence and plan carefully (with support when it's necessary), you will have moved from listening to team decisions to influencing them. That's exactly the position you should be in when you attend any meeting.

That doesn't mean you'll need to influence decisions all the time. When things are going well, you can sit back and enjoy the process knowing you have made a contribution to your child's success. It's one of the well-deserved benefits of becoming knowledgeable.

Carrying a genuine belief in your child's success, supported by intense services, will have its positive influence as well. As you learned in chapter 1, it will allow your child to be productive and successful at school and in other areas of life. You'll have the same influence when you carry a genuine belief in your child's success, supported by appropriate accommodations, if your child has a physical or mental impairment (discussed in chapter 12).

If you go online and read the biographies of high functioning adults with LD (or those with physical or mental impairments), you'll find that productivity and a belief in success are common characteristics. That's what you're aiming for and that's what you can help to create for your child. Your genuine belief, coupled with intensive services (or appropriate 504 services), is the cornerstone for making that happen.

You may be thinking that intense services will be difficult to obtain. Remember that you won't ask for intense services until you have evidence of regression supported by other relevant information. You will also have an advocate or private evaluator with you in key meetings when you make those requests. Then, use an IEE, mediation or a due process hearing or your state's complaint process if you need to, to make sure your child's unique needs are met. You can feel very confident about the outcome of your meetings when you use this approach. It's *your* prescription for success. Use it along with your genuine belief in your child's success, to help your child become productive and successful in life.

Appendix I:
Sample Letters

Sample Letter 1: Requesting a Special Education Evaluation

[Parents: Keep a copy of your letter for your own files.]

Mary Smith
327 Scantic Drive
Northampton, MA 01062

February 12, 2015

Mr. John Hicks
Administrator of Special Education
45 Main Street
Northampton, MA 01062

Dear Mr. Hicks:

I'm writing to request a special education evaluation for my daughter Jessica, who is in first grade at Meadowbrook School. Jessica struggled in kindergarten learning to write and to recognize her letters. Her first grade teacher, Mrs. Know, also told me at our recent parent conference that Jessica was having great difficulty learning the sounds of letters and is not yet able to blend letters. She still has difficulty forming her letters when she writes.

Jessica is falling further behind her peers. I believe that an evaluation now will help us better understand her needs and determine if she qualifies for special education. I understand that you require my written consent to evaluate Jessica. Please consider this letter my consent to evaluate. I would also appreciate receiving a copy of the school district's testing two days before Jessica's scheduled evaluation meeting.

I can be reached during the day at 423-739-2006 or after 4:00 P.M. at 413-739-4797 if you need further information. I look forward to your response at the earliest possible date.

Sincerely,

Mary Smith

Sample Letter 2: Requesting a Special Education Evaluation (if you have had your child evaluated privately)

[Parents: Keep a copy of your letter for your own files.]

Nancy Gilbert
15 Main Street
Hadley, MA 01062

January 25, 2015

Ms. Janice Brown
Administrator of Special Education
45 Main Street
Northampton, MA 01062

Dear Ms. Brown:

I'm writing to request a special education evaluation for our son Michael, who is in second grade at Mapleshade School. We have been concerned about Michael's progress since he was in kindergarten. Ms. Staples, Michael's second-grade teacher, told me at our recent parent—teacher conference that he was performing well below his classmates in the areas of reading, writing, and spelling.

I'm enclosing the results of a private evaluation completed at University of Massachusetts Medical Center that we would like to discuss at our evaluation meeting. Dr. John Chase, who completed the evaluation on Michael, will attend the meeting with us.

I understand that you require my written consent to evaluate Michael. Please consider this letter my consent to evaluate. I can be reached during the day at 423-739-2006 or after 4:00 P.M. at 413-739- 4797 if you need further information. I would appreciate receiving a copy of any testing by the school district two days before Michael's scheduled evaluation meeting. I look forward to your response at the earliest possible date.

Sincerely,

Nancy Gilbert

Sample Letter 3: Requesting an Independent Evaluation

[Parents: Keep a copy of your letter for your own files.]

Martha Cox
45 Village Lane
Amherst, MA 01062

February 13, 2015

Ms. Janice Green
Administrator of Special Education
65 Young Street
Amherst, MA 01062

Dear Ms. Green:

I am writing regarding our son, Jason Cox, who is in fourth grade at Tallmadge School. My husband and I attended an initial evaluation meeting for Jason on February 6, 2014. We are requesting an IEE at public expense for the following reason (s):

The evaluation did not include testing for [name the area not included here, such as testing for a processing disorder, testing for ADD, language testing, or neuropsychological testing. Or, you can say something more general, such as the evaluation did not accurately reflect your child's unique needs or was not comprehensive enough.]

Please forward the school district's guidelines for independent evaluations and a list of the district's approved evaluators. We understand that we can select someone who is not on the approved list.

I can be reached during the day at 423-739-2006 or after 4:00 P.M. at 413-739-4797 if you need further information. I look forward to your response at the earliest possible date.

Sincerely,

Martha Cox

Sample Letter 4: Informing the School District That a Professional Will Accompany You to a Team Meeting

[Parents: Keep a copy of your letter for your own files.]

Nancy Brace
13 Sumner Avenue
Springfield, MA 01076

March 24, 2015

Mr. John Blackwell
Administrator of Special Education
151 State Street
Springfield, MA 01042

Dear Mr. Blackwell:

I am writing to let you know that Ms. Shelia White, [identify the professional. It might be a special education advocate or a psychologist in private practice] will attend the team meeting about our son, Michael Brace, on April 28, 2013.

I can be reached at 413-733-5732 between 8:30 A.M. and 4:00 P.M. and at 413-737-2478 after 5:00 P.M. if you have questions.

I look forward to a productive team meeting.

Sincerely,

Nancy Brace

Sample Letter 5: Requesting Permission to Observe Your District's Self-Contained LD Program

[Parents: Keep a copy of your letter for your own files.]

Linda Dodge
76 Hazelwood Avenue
Springfield, MA 01076

March 2, 2015

Dr. Lisa Fontaine
Administrator of Special Education
22 Cottage Street
Springfield, MA 01042

Dear Dr. Fontaine:

I recently attended an IEP meeting about my son, Timothy, who is in fifth grade at Center School. Timothy was recommended for placement in Center School's self-contained LD program next year. I am requesting permission for Dr. Nancy Rice, who is a special education supervisor in private practice, to observe the self-contained program.

Please forward any documents I may need to sign as well as possible observation dates. Dr. Rice may need to complete more than one observation to have a comprehensive view of the self-contained program.

I can be reached at 413-733-4260 between 8:30 A.M. and 4:00 P.M. and at 413-737-2985 after 5:00 P.M. if you have questions.

I look forward to your response at the earliest possible date.

Sincerely,

Linda Dodge

Appendix II:
Dropping Your Child from Services

In chapter 5, I discussed finding an advocate who could support you if you knew that the district might recommend dropping your child at a re-evaluation meeting (see chapter 5 for more on re-evaluation meetings).

You and the advocate should review three central questions to determine if your child is ready to be dropped from services.

- Are your child's skills close to or at grade level?

You may recall from chapter 2 that you will want standard scores, percentiles, or scaled scores from standardized tests at or above 90, 25 and 8 respectively (the team may consider scores of 85, 16, and 7 to indicate that your child has average performance).

- Is your child independent in her skills?

Your child should be able to use a skill with a minimum of assistance from a professional. Spelling and fluency (performing a skill for speed and accuracy) are the skills that will be the most difficult to master. When I refer to fluency here, I'm referring to fluency in reading, writing, or math. You'll want to know if your child can use the spellcheck feature on a word processor or other technology and that she is independent when reviewing her writing for spelling errors. Likewise, you'll want to know if your child's fluency is at a point that it does not cause high levels of frustration or anxiety, and that she can complete homework assignments in a reasonable amount of time.

Your child should also be skilled at using strategies for writing stories, reports, or term papers, as well as strategies to edit her work.

- Will your child need accommodations if she is dropped from special education?

If so, she may be eligible for a Section 504 plan (see chapter 12 for more on 504 plans).

Your advocate should attend your child's meeting with you. Their role in the meeting will be to make sure the team considers the three central questions before dropping your child from services. If a 504 meeting is needed, I also recommend that the advocate attend that meeting with you.

Appendix III:
Home and Hospital Services

Meeting Your State's Regulations

You learned in chapter 12 that your child may be eligible for home and hospital services if he's expected to be out of school for less than six months. Let's look more closely at what you'll need to do for him to receive home or hospital services.

The most important thing you'll need is a letter from a doctor stating your child's diagnosis and that he will be out for more than the number of days required by your state's regulations. Ten days is the standard used in most states.

If your child is expected to be out more than 10 days (or the number of days allowed by your state's regulations), it will allow him to receive tutoring until he's ready to return to school. If he has a chronic condition such asthma or chronic fatigue and he will be absent frequently, it's usual to wave the number of days allowed by your state. This means there should be no waiting period before home tutoring services start.

How to Request Home Tutoring

The superintendent's office (it may be called a board of education) in your district can tell you who to contact if your child will require home tutoring. When you contact that person, you can find out the number of days your child must be out of school to qualify for tutoring.

Your district will require a letter from your doctor or specialist requesting home tutoring. Find out if the district has a letter that explains what a doctor must submit. If they do, you can forward it to your doctor.

If there is no letter explaining what a doctor must submit, ask what should be in a letter so you can give the information to your doctor's office. Also, make sure to let the district know if your child has a chronic condition. This will require a different letter.

The most frequent delay in starting home tutoring is the amount of time it takes for your doctor to send a letter to the school district. Start that process as soon as you know your child will be out for more than the required number of days and follow up every few days until a letter has been received by the school district.

The person in charge of home and hospital services will need to receive that letter before home tutoring can start. Also make sure to follow up with the school district if a home tutor has been assigned to your child and you haven't received a phone call to start tutoring.

How to Request Hospital Services

The person in charge of home and hospital services can also tell you the requirements for tutoring if your child will be in a hospital. It's usual for school districts to have an arrangement with local hospitals to provide tutoring during the time a child is in the hospital. Notify the district in advance of your child's stay if you're able to, or as soon after his admission as possible.

Your child may also need a period of tutoring at home after he has left the hospital. Let the person in charge of home and hospital services know when that will take place and follow the procedures required. Ideally, there should be no interruption in tutoring services from hospital to home.

Appendix IV:
Considering Remedial Programs If Your Child Does Not Qualify for Special Education

This information covers remedial programs listed at the end chapter 2. You can consider a remedial program, but I recommend investigating it thoroughly before you make a decision to use it.

I also recommend using an advocate for your initial contact when investigating a remedial program. You can review this information with them as you prepare for your meeting.

The following are elements of a well-designed remedial program:

- The program is research-based.
- The program is used with fidelity (the way it's intended).
- Children are seen four or five times per week.
- Children receive a minimum of 45 to 60 minutes per day for reading, 75 to 90 minutes per day for reading and writing combined, 45 to 60 minutes per day for math, and 15 to 20 minutes per day for fluency.
- Progress is monitored frequently—at least monthly—using objective measures.
- Parents receive feedback about their child's progress at the time report cards are issued.
- Parents receive objective information showing their child's progress over time.
- Group size is kept to a maximum of four students.

I recommend waiting about six months (two marking periods) to see how your child responds. If the program is helping, you will see progress. Your child should be more relaxed and enthusiastic about school.

Move on to consider other options mentioned in chapter 2 if you're not seeing those changes. If the program does not have the elements above when you first review it, you will want to consider a private option.

Glossary of Special Education and Assessment Terms

A

accommodations: Changes that are made in testing that do not alter what a test measures. The purpose of an accommodation is to allow a child with a disability to demonstrate his knowledge, not the effect of his disability. An example might be a child with a reading disability receiving extra time to take a reading test.

annual review: A meeting held each year once a student has an IEP. Its purpose is to review progress on the goals and objectives in an IEP.

attention deficit hyperactivity disorder (ADHD): A disorder in which a student displays highly active and impulsive behavior.

B

behavior management program (BMP): A program developed for a student whose behavior affects his learning and/or the learning of others. For the student with a learning disability, the most frequent behavior that requires a BMP occurs when the student has ADHD combined with LD.

C

complaint process: A process used by states to address concerns by parents about their child's special education program. Complaints are frequently filed when a school district isn't providing a program or service in an IEP. It requires a written document describing the parent's disagreement with the school district and a proposed solution.

composite score: A score that combines several subtests on a test to get an average score. For example, it might be used to combine spelling and written expression subtests to obtain a composite score for written language.

curriculum-based assessment (CBA): Refers to models of assessment that are aligned with a school's curriculum. A defining characteristic of CBAs is that assessments are given frequently and the results are used to make decisions about instruction.

curriculum-based measurement (CBM): A specific form of CBA that uses repeated measures from the student's curriculum to evaluate the effectiveness of instruction and to make instructional changes.

D

district test: A test given by a school district to evaluate the effectiveness of instruction and/or student progress. District tests are usually given to a large segment of the school population, for example, all elementary grades. Parents receive the results of district evaluations when they're used to evaluate student progress.

due process hearing: A formal process to resolve disputes between parents and school districts. A due process hearing involves presenting evidence and calling witnesses to testify in the presence of a hearing officer. It is the hearing officer who makes a final decision to resolve disputes, and this decision is binding on both parties.

duel discrepancy: A term used when two sources of information confirm that a student's progress is poor. For example, a duel discrepancy is present if the results of progress monitoring (the testing component of RTI) and a standardized achievement test confirm that a student's progress is poor.

F

functional skill: Skills such as a student's communication, social skills, behavior, or motor skills. They may be part of a student's IEP or may be given as a separate service.

I

independent educational evaluation (IEE): An evaluation by a professional who is not associated with a school district. It's used when a parent disagrees with a school district evaluation. There is no cost to a parent for an IEE.

individual educational program (IEP): A document that describes the program that will be used for teaching and for following a student's progress. IEPs are written once a student is found eligible for special education services. They're reviewed annually.

initial evaluation: A first evaluation to determine whether a student is eligible for special education services.

Individuals with Disabilities Education Act (IDEA): The federal special education statute and regulations that all states must follow to provide early intervention, special education, and related service for children with disabilities.

L

learning disability (LD): A disorder that affects the ability to understand or use spoken or written language. It includes difficulties with listening, thinking, reading, writing, spelling, and doing mathematical calculations.

M

measurable goal: A goal that is written with a number or percent of attainment. Measurable goals are used in special education to predict a student's progress over a period of time, such as a school year. They're useful because they provide objective information documenting a student's progress.

mediation: A procedure to resolve disputes between parents and a school district. Mediation can be beneficial if the parent and the school district are close to resolving their differences. An example would be a dispute over the amount of time a child should receive services. There is no cost for mediation.

N

No Child Left Behind (NCLB): A federal law enacted in 2001 to hold school districts accountable for high standards of student achievement. All children, including children with disabilities, are tested yearly in third through eighth grades in reading and mathematics. They are tested once in high school in the same skill areas. All children are also tested three times in science: once each at the elementary, middle, and high school levels. Parents receive the results of these tests.

P

pattern of strengths and weaknesses (PSW): One of the methods that states may use to determine eligibility for special education. A team using this method will look at a student's performance (such as report card grades or teacher comments) as well as achievement on standardized tests to determine eligibility.

percentile: Used frequently in special education testing to indicate how a student compares to peers at their age or grade level. For example, a percentile of 74 will tell a parent that their child has scored the same as or better than 74 percent of the students who took the same test.

present levels of academic achievement and functional performance (PLOP): A description in an IEP that states what a child can do now. Academic achievement refers to performance in subjects like reading, writing, and math. Functional performance refers to activities such as your child's behavior, social skills, and communication skills.

private evaluation: An evaluation by a professional not associated with a school district and paid for by a parent. It's used by parents who wish to have a comprehensive picture of their child's skills and ability or if there is a dispute over a child's services.

processing disorder: A general term used to describe a variety of disorders that affect the way the brain processes information. A student with a processing disorder may have difficulty on tasks that require remembering information over short or long periods, being able to read quickly and accurately, or being able to solve problems in mathematics. Most experts believe that a processing disorder points to the underlying cause of a learning disability.

progress monitoring: A method of monitoring student progress using standardized tests that are given frequently. It includes adjustments in instruction to improve performance.

R

reading fluency: A student's reading rate and accuracy as well as their expression. The sign of a fluent reader is their ability to read quickly, accurately, and effortlessly. Fluent readers are able to read words as whole words automatically, with little attention to how words appear.

regression: A term used in special education to indicate that a student's standard scores on a standardized achievement test have dropped compared to previous years.

re-evaluation: Also called a triennial evaluation. This is an evaluation every three years for students with IEPs. The intent of a re-evaluation is to re-peat a student's original testing. In practice, most re-evaluations focus on formal testing of the student's achievement and/or functional skills.

response to intervention (RTI): A model used to identify students (typically in the early grades) who are at risk of failure. It includes monitoring progress frequently and adjusting instruction to improve performance.

S

scaled score: A conversion of a student's raw score on a test to a common scale. Scaled scores are used with standardized achievement tests in special education and range between 1 and 19 with 10 as an average score. Because it's an objective measure and is an equal interval scale, parents can use scaled scores to compare their child's growth over time.

Section 504 of the Rehabilitation Acts of 1973 (referred to as Section 504): Referred to as an equal access law because its intent is to provide students with disabilities access to programs and activities in a public school available to all students. To qualify for Section 504, a student must have a physical or mental impairment that substantially limits one or more major life activities.

Major life activities include functions such as caring for oneself, performing manual tasks, seeing, hearing, speaking, breathing, walking, learning, communicating, and working.

severe discrepancy method: A method that looks at the correlation (relationship) between an IQ test (usually the total score) and a total score or cluster score from an achievement test. It's one of the methods used to determine eligibility for special education. A severe discrepancy can't be used alone to determine eligibility.

standardized: A procedure for creating, administering, scoring, summarizing, and interpreting tests results that follow a specific set of rules.

standard deviation: Used in testing to tell how spread-out a distribution is from the mean or average score. In most achievement and intelligence tests, the pattern of this distribution follows a normal curve called a normal distribution. In a normal distribution, most of the scores are concentrated around the center (mean) and decrease (deviate) by the same amount on either side of the mean.

standard score: Indicates how far above or below the average (mean) an individual score falls. Standard scores have a common scale in which the average score is typically 100 with a range of 55 to 145. Many achievement and intelligence tests in public schools use standard scores.

T

tier: Term used in conjunction with RTI. It refers to the intensity of service a child receives and is typically offered at three levels (tiers), from least to most intensive.

W

Wechsler Individual Achievement Test (WIAT III): A comprehensive test of achievement that measures a broad range of academic skills. Norms extend from preschool to adult.

Wechsler Intelligence Scale for Children(WISC-IV): A widely recognized and used intelligence test for children ages 6 to 16. It provides insights into a child's cognitive functioning. The results are often used to recommend strategies for the child in the classroom.

Woodcock–Johnson Tests of Achievement (WJ III): A comprehensive test of achievement that measures a wide variety of academic skills. Norms extend from preschool to adult.

work samples: Samples of a student's daily work and includes seatwork as well as tests and quiz results. Parents can use work samples to support their request for eligibility to special education or increasing their child's services.

References

Advocates for Special Education. 2015. "Find and Advocate or Attorney." Advocates for Special Education. Accessed January 18. http://www.advocatesforspecialeducation.com/find.html.

Advocates for Special Education. 2015. "Guidelines for Choosing an Advocate or Attorney." Advocates for Special Education. Accessed January 15. http://advocatesforspecialeducation.com/guidelines.html.

Bateman, Barbara D., and Cynthia Herr. 2006. "Writing Measurable IEP Goals and Objectives: IEP Resources." Attainment Company. http://www.attainmentcompany.com/sites/default/files/pdf/sample/WMIEP_Sample.pdf.

Colorado Department of Education. 2008. "Guidelines for Identifying Students with Specific Learning Disabilities." Colorado Department of Education. http://www.cde.state.co.us/sites/default/files/documents/cdesped/download/pdf/sld_guidelines.pdf.

Center for Parent Information and Resources. 2015. "All about the IEP." Center for Parent Information and Resources. Accessed January 18. http://www.parentcenterhub.org/repository/iep/.

Center for Parent Information and Resources. 2014. "Subpart D of the Part B Regulations: Evaluations, Eligibility, IEPs, and Placement." Center for Parent Information and Resources. Accessed November 20. http://www.parentcenterhub.org/repository/partb-subpartd/.

Center for Parent Information and Resources. 2014. "School Accommodation and Modification Ideas for Students Who Receive Special Education Services." Center for Parent Information and

Resources. Accessed September 15. http://www.parentcenterhub. org/repository/accommodation.

New York State Special Education Department. 2010. "Annual Goals, Short-Term Instructional Objectives and/or Benchmarks." New York State Special Education Department. http://www.p12. nysed.gov/specialed/publications/iepguidance/annual.htm.

South Lane School District. 2015. "504 Resources: Section 504 Sample Accommodations and Modifications." South Lane School District. Accessed January 25. https://d2ct263enury6r.cloudfront. net/1AE6yHL9wFq2ovxtJcqxUKBVCwPbpvpBzzjnUxC3tJZ-BIIEs.pdf.

US Department of Education. 2010. "Guidelines for Educators and Administrators for Implementing Section 504 of the Rehabilitation Act of 1973-Subpart D." US Department of Education. https://doe.sd.gov/oess/documents/sped_section504_Guidelines.pdf.

Wrightslaw. 2015. "Wrightslaw Yellow Pages for Kids." Wrightslaw. Accessed January 5. http://www.yellowpagesforkids.com/.

Index

www.ingramcontent.com/pod-product-compliance
Lightning Source LLC
Chambersburg PA
CBHW050126280326
41933CB00010B/1261